DIRT SIMPLE®

PEDAL STEEL GUITAR

BY
JOHN HARTIN
AND CHET HARTIN

I0804484

Online Audio www.melbay.com/30706MEB

WWW.MELBAY.COM

Introduction

The steel guitar and country music go back a long way. From its roots in Hawaiian music to the addition of pedals in the 1940s. No other guitar so closely emulates the human voice, its characteristic sound can be heard on many of the greatest country hits.

This book will teach you how to play several well-known songs on the pedal steel guitar. We hope it will also help you to play in tune, and pick correctly.

Acknowledgements

Special thanks go out to our family. We would also like to thank Dann Tincher, Jacinda Beth, Stuart Moody, and Gordon Hartin for all the additional help in completeting this project.

Many thanks,

John & Chet Hartin

Table Of Contents

Reading Tablature and Picking

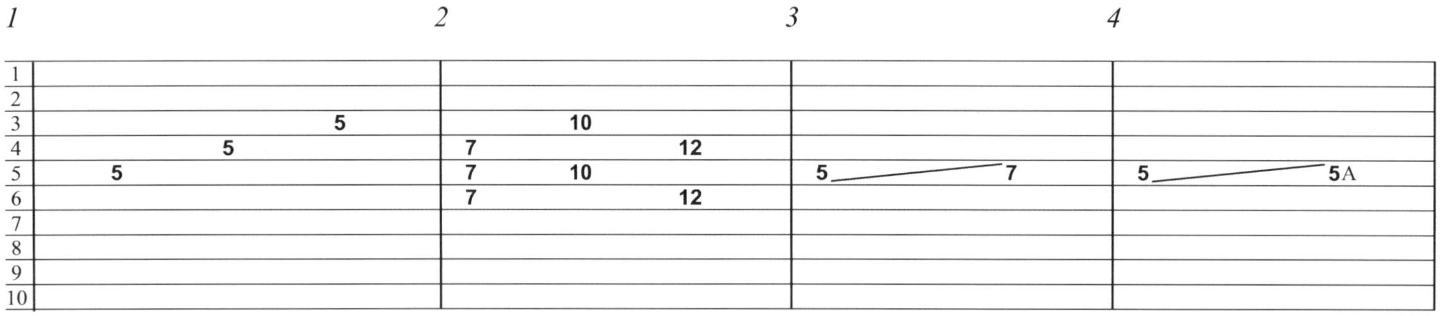

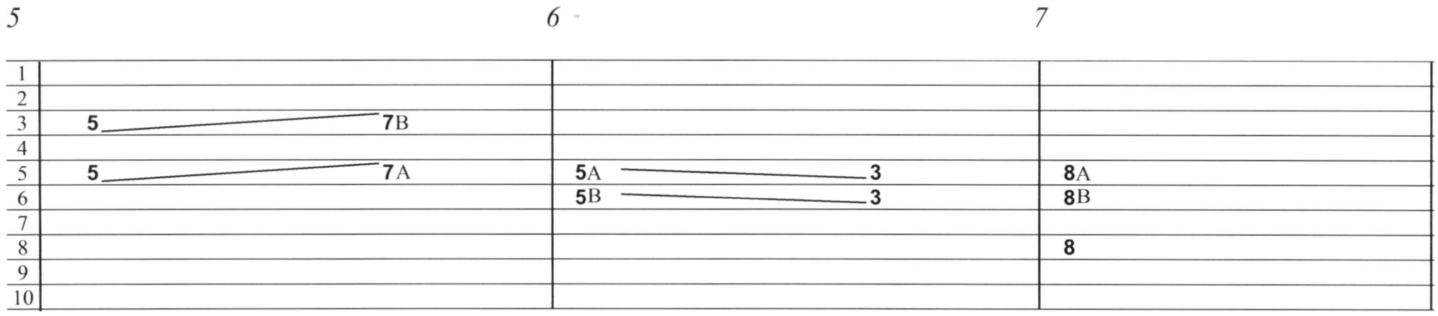

Example 1: Pick the 5th string with the bar on the 5th fret. Then pick the 4th string with the bar on the 5th fret, and then finally pick the 3rd string with the bar on the 5th fret. These are all single notes picked in order from left-to-right.

Example 2: Pick the 4th, 5th, and 6th strings all at the same time with the bar on the 7th fret, then pick the 3rd and 5th strings with the bar moved up to the 10th fret and finally pick the 4th and 6th strings together with the bar on the 12th fret.

Example 3: Pick the 5th string with the bar on the 5th fret, and then slide the bar up to the 7th fret without picking the strings again. Also notice the **Glissando** sign - this indicates a slide up or down or pedal up or down.

Example 4: Pick the 5th string with the bar on the 5th fret and then push pedal A while the note is still ringing. Notice when there is a connector line, do not pick the string again.

Example 5: Pick the 3rd and 5th strings with the bar on the 5th fret, then slide the bar to the 7th fret without picking the notes again - by the time you reach the 7th fret, push the A and B pedals down.

Example 6: Pick the 5th and 6th strings at the same time with the A and B pedals down, lift your foot off the pedals and slide down to the 3rd fret without picking the notes again.

Example 7: This is nothing but a two-pedal combination. Pick the 5th, 6th and 8th string with the bar on the 8th fret.

Picking

1. The picking hand will pick the strings. Use a plastic pick on your thumb and metal finger picks on your index and middle finger.
2. Use the thumb pick when picking notes away from your body and use the middle finger when picking notes towards your body.

Pedals and Grips

Your pedal steel will likely have 3 pedals - these are identified as A, B, and C (from left-to-right). In other books, you may see these listed as pedal 1,2,3 - which is the common "Emmons" setup. If your steel has the pedals reversed, this is the "Day" setup. If your steel has 4 pedals, disregard the first one as A will likely be pedal 2. This book will only use 2 knee levers identified as E & F. Your steel may vary, but these will typically be the Left-Knee lever on the right side (LKR), and the Left-Knee lever on the left side (LKL).

Floor Pedals

E9 Tuning

	A	B	C
F♯			
D♯			
G♯		A	
E			F♯
B	C♯		C♯
G♯		A	
F♯			
E			
D			
B	C♯		

Knee Levers

	E	F
F♯		
D♯		
G♯		
E	E♭	F
B		
G♯		
F♯		
E	E♭	F
D		
B		

Grips

There are 4 main right-hand positions for the pedal steel. These are called **grips**, since your hand grips the strings. Grips represent 4 ways to play the same chord on the same fret. They can be played on any fret of the pedal steel, though of course the key will change as you move the bar. These grips are going to be critcal to your pedal steel journey. Play the lowest note with your thumb followed by your index finger; below your middle finger should play the highest note. Be sure to memorize all four! The example below shows the 4 grips or positions on the pedal steel in the key of E. Feel free to grab your bar, and try these out at different frets.

String	*1*	*2*	*3*	*4*
1				
2				
3				0
4			0	0
5		0	0	0
6	0	0	0	
7				
8	0	0		
9				
10	0			

Positions and Blocking

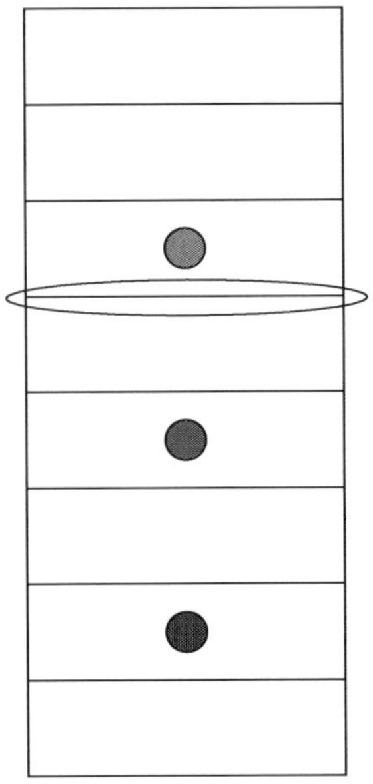

When finding your note, hold the bar directly over the fret marking, and not in-between frets in the "box".

Blocking

An essential technique for playing the pedal steel is **blocking**. Blocking means physically stopping a note from ringing when going to the next note. The traditional method is to roll the edge of your picking hand to physically stop the note. A modern method is pick-blocking where a pick physically stops the note from ringing. In the exercise below try both methods. Blocking takes time to develop and most players use one method or the other. Choose the method that works best for you.

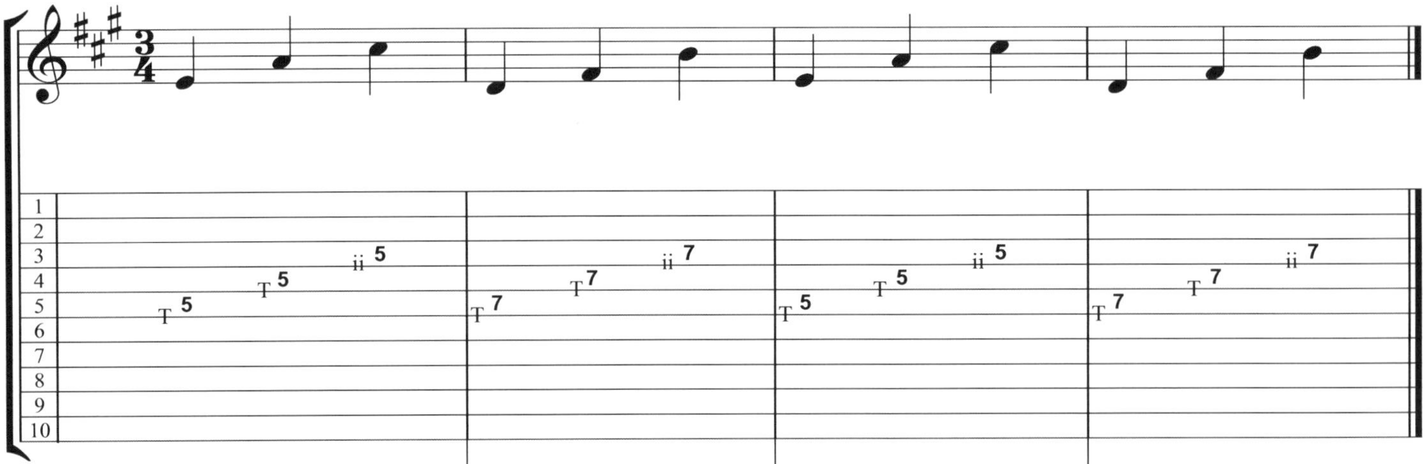

"Block" each note with the edge of your picking hand before attacking the next note.	"Block" each note with your pick.	"Block" each note with your pick.	"Block" each note with the edge of your picking hand.

T = Thumb
i = First Finger
ii = Second Finger

Bile Them Cabbage Down

This tune is often played on the fiddle, but it's mighty fun to play on the pedal steel guitar! Note the use of the B pedal, make sure it is pressed down before playing the note.

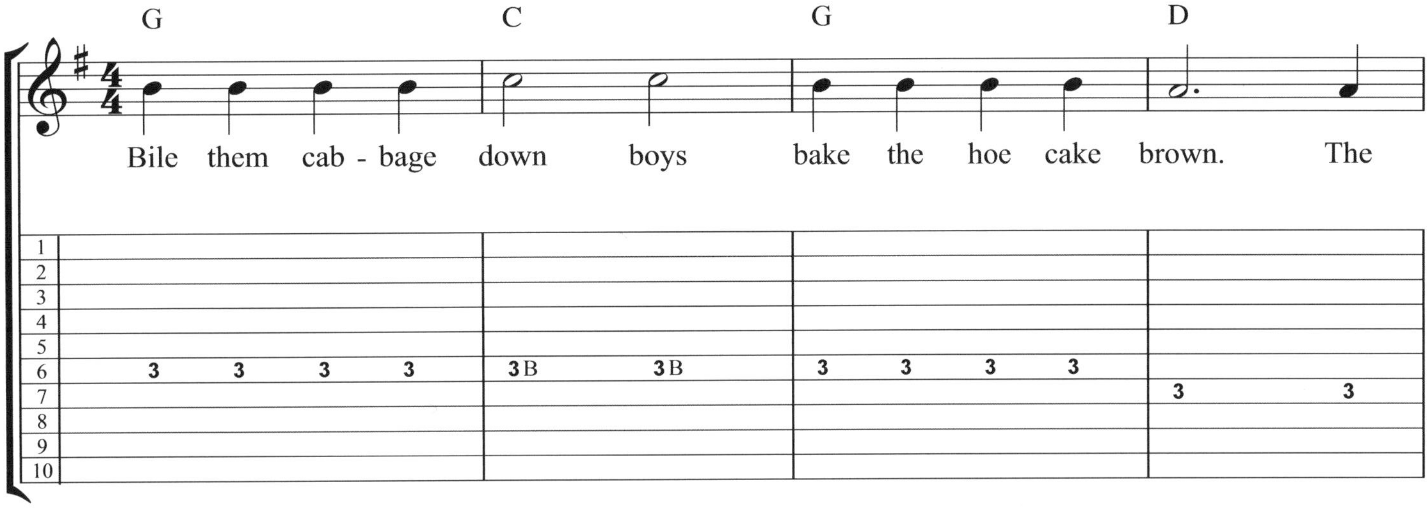

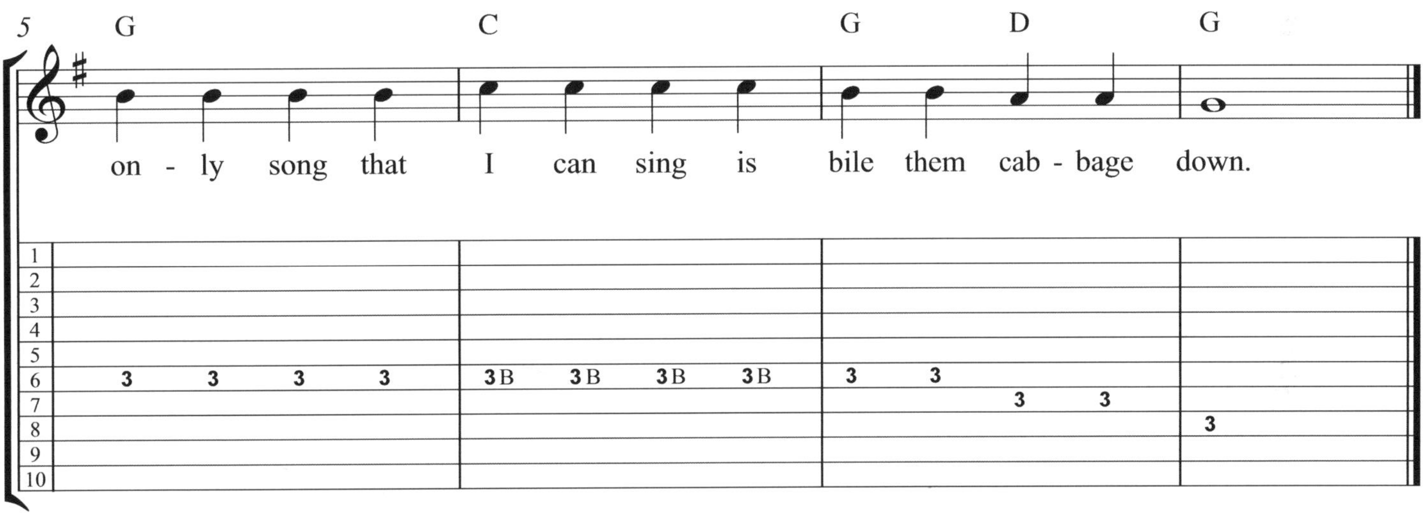

Went up on the mountain
Just to give my horn a blow
Thought I heard my true love say
Yonder comes my beau

Took my gal to the blacksmith shop
To have her mouth made small
She turned around a time or two
And swallowd shop and all

Possum in a Simmon tree
Raccoon on the ground
Raccoon says you son-of-a-gun
Shake some Simmon's down

Someone stole my old 'coon dog
Wish they'd bring him back
He chased the big hogs through the fence
And the little ones through the crack

Once I had an old gray mule
His name was Simon Slick
He'd roll his eyes and back his ears
And how that mule would kick

How that mule would kick
He kicked with his dying breath
He shoved his hind feet down his throat
And kicked himself to death

When the Saints Go Marching In

Elvis Presley, Fats Domino, and Louis Armstrong, are just a few of the artists who have recorded the timeless “When the Saints Go Marching In”. Note the use of the B pedal.

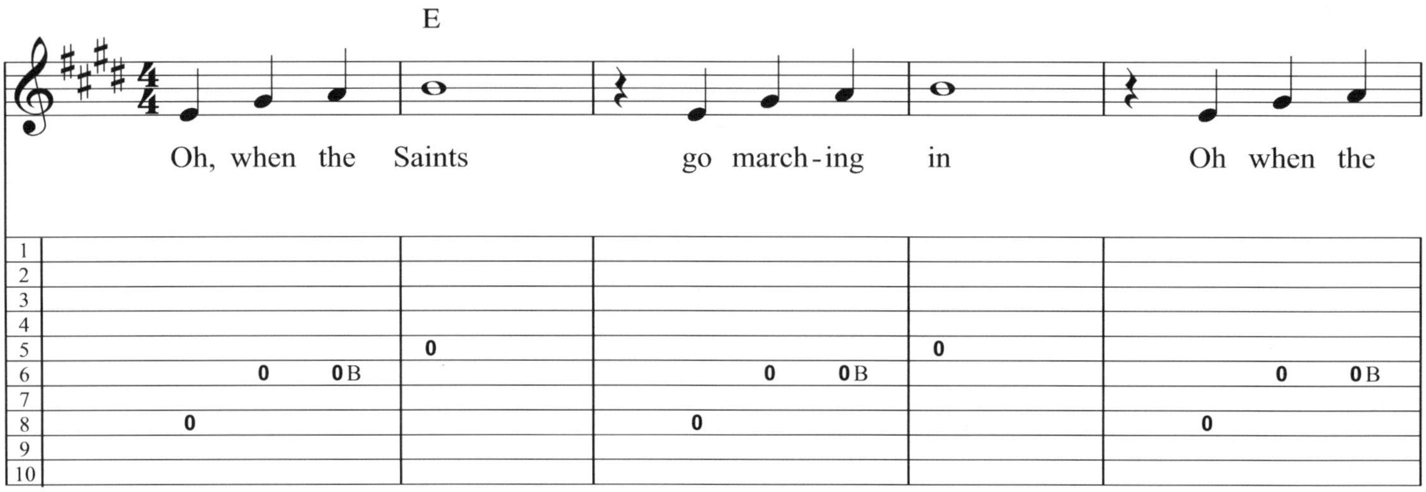

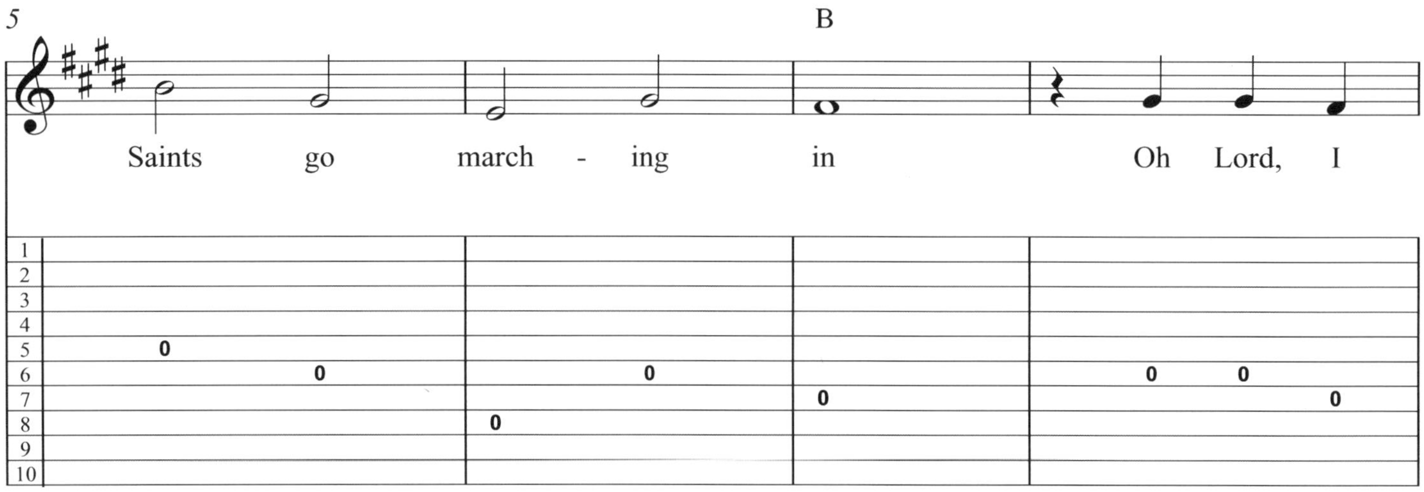

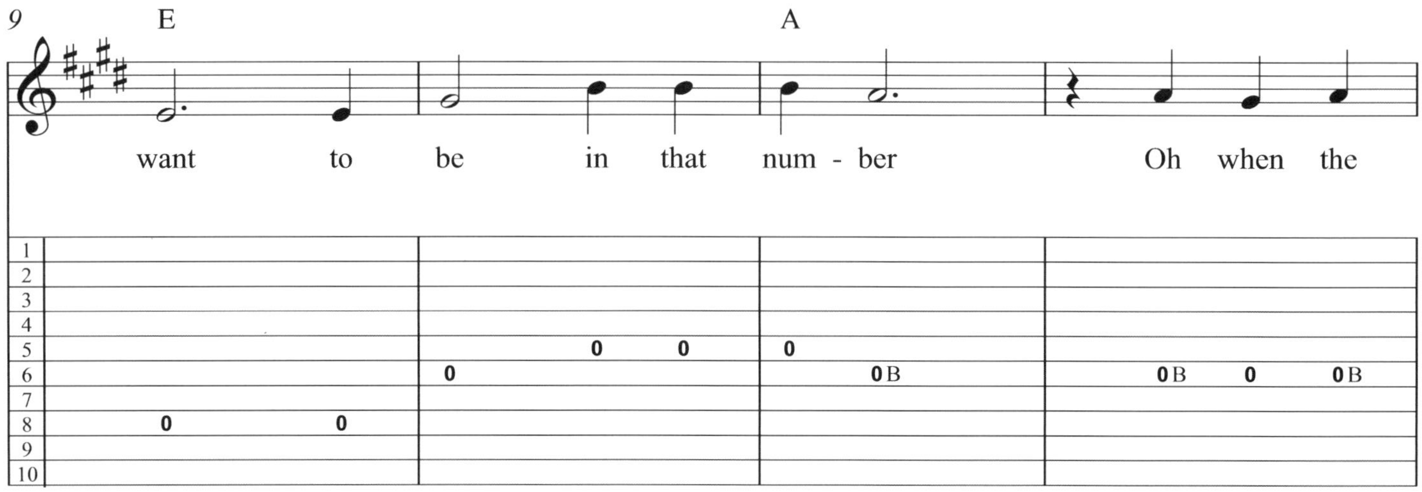

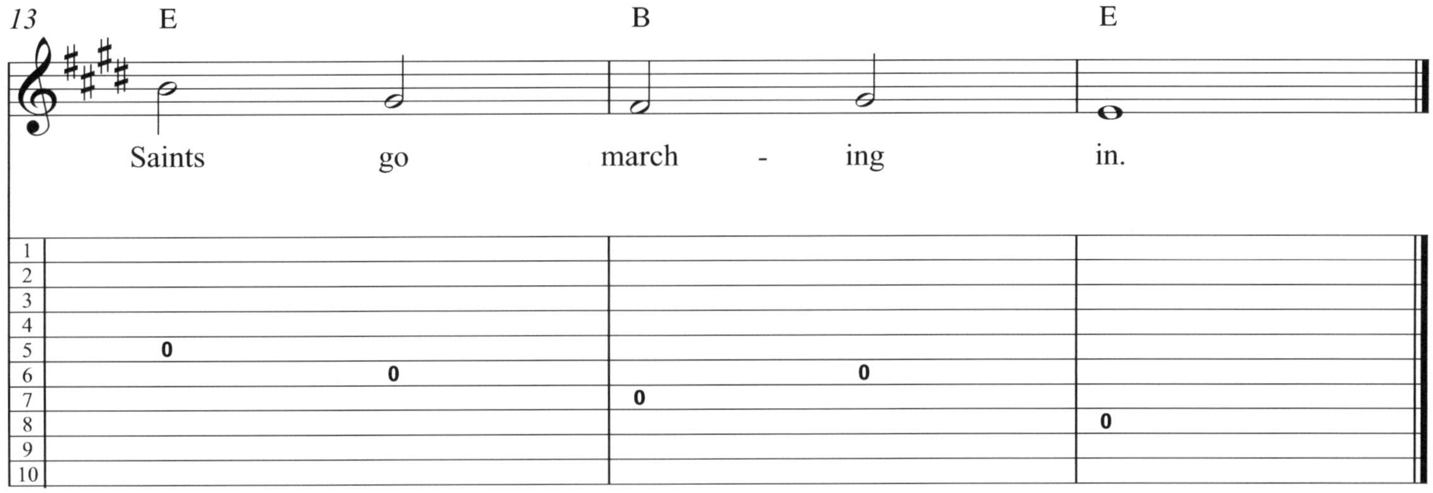

We are all traveling in the footsteps
Of those that'd come before
And we'll all be reunited
On that new and sunlit shore

And when the sun refuses to shine
When the sun refuses to shine
Lord, how I want to be in that number
When the Saints go marching in

When the trumpet sounds its call
When the trumpet sounds its call
Oh, how I want be in that number
When the trumpet sounds its call

Now some say, some say this world of trouble
Is the only world we'll ever see
But I'm waiting for that morning
When the new world is revealed

Oh, when the new world is revealed
Oh, when the new world is revealed
Lord, how I want to be there on that morning
When the new world is revealed

Bury Me Beneath the Willow

"Bury Me Beneath the Willow" has been performed by many country artists, including Dolly Parton, The Carter Family, Allison Krauss, and many others. Note the use of the A and B pedals and carefully "block" each note.

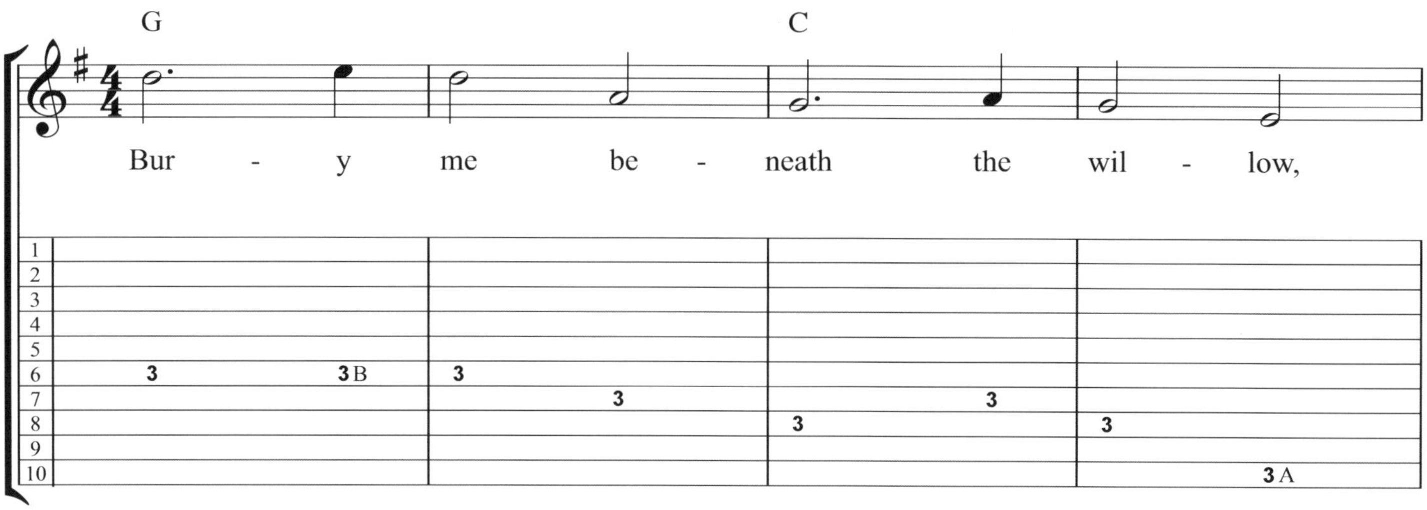

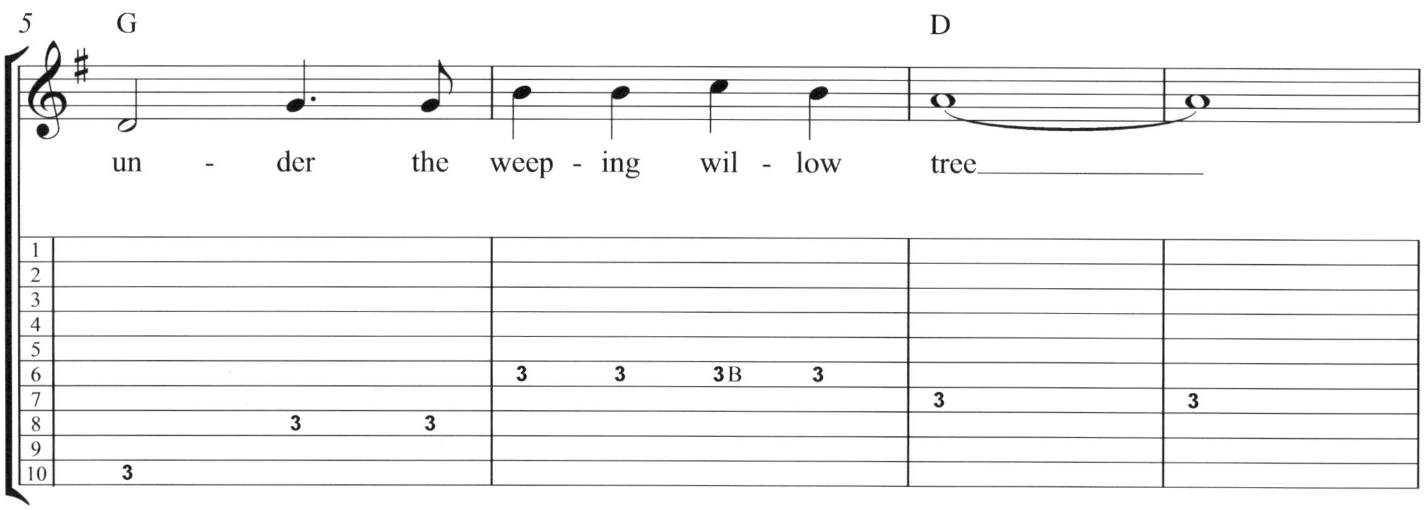

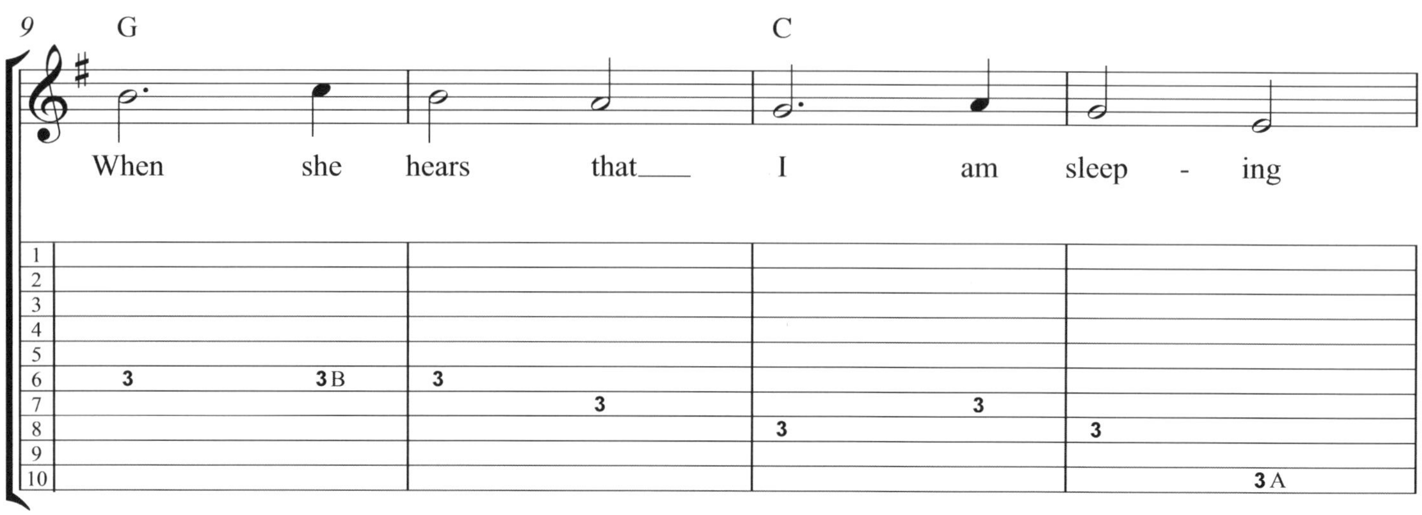

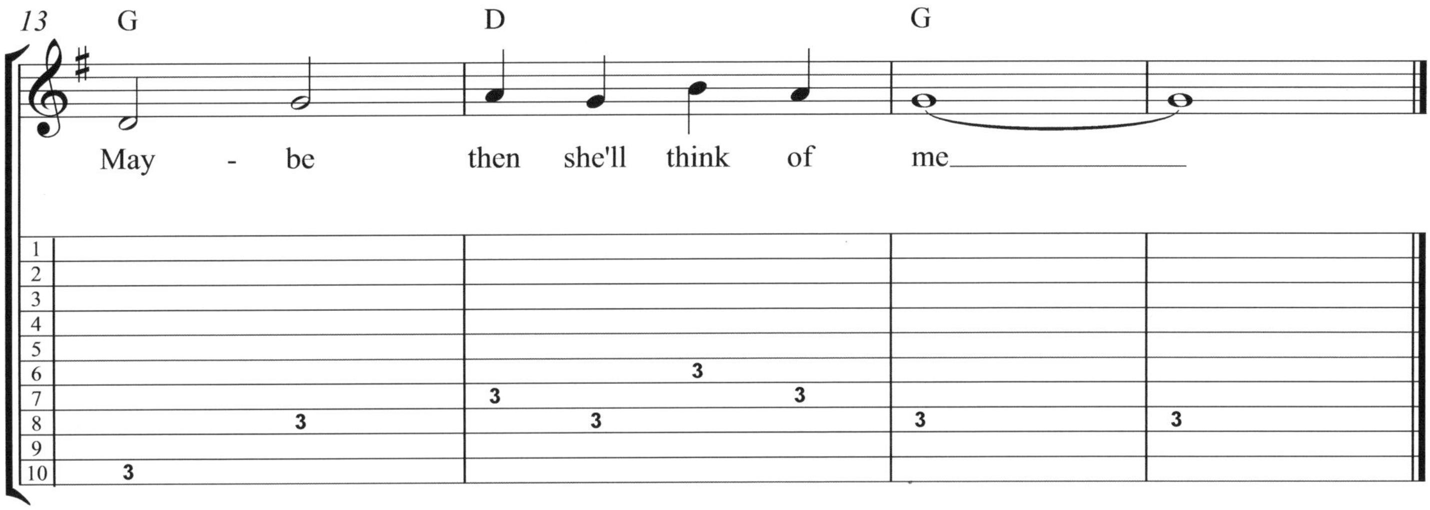

My heart is sad I am lonely
For the only one I love
When shall I see her oh no never
'Til we meet in heaven above

She told me that she dearly loved me
How could I believe it untrue
Until the angels softly whispered
She will prove untrue to you

Tomorrow was to be our wedding
God oh God where can she be
She's out a courting with another
And no longer cares for me

On Top of Old Smoky

"On Top of Old Smoky" is an American Folksong about the Smoky Mountains. It was recorded by the legendary Hank Williams, Burl Ives, and Gene Autry. Watch measure 5 as it starts with the fourth fret with the A pedal and goes back down to the 3rd fret.

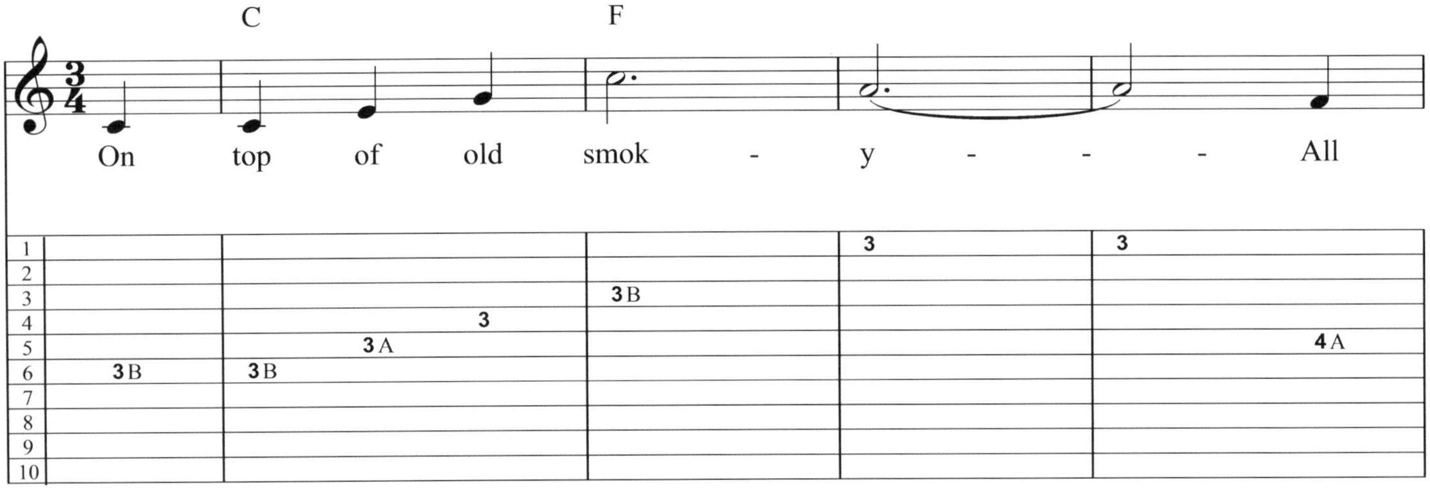

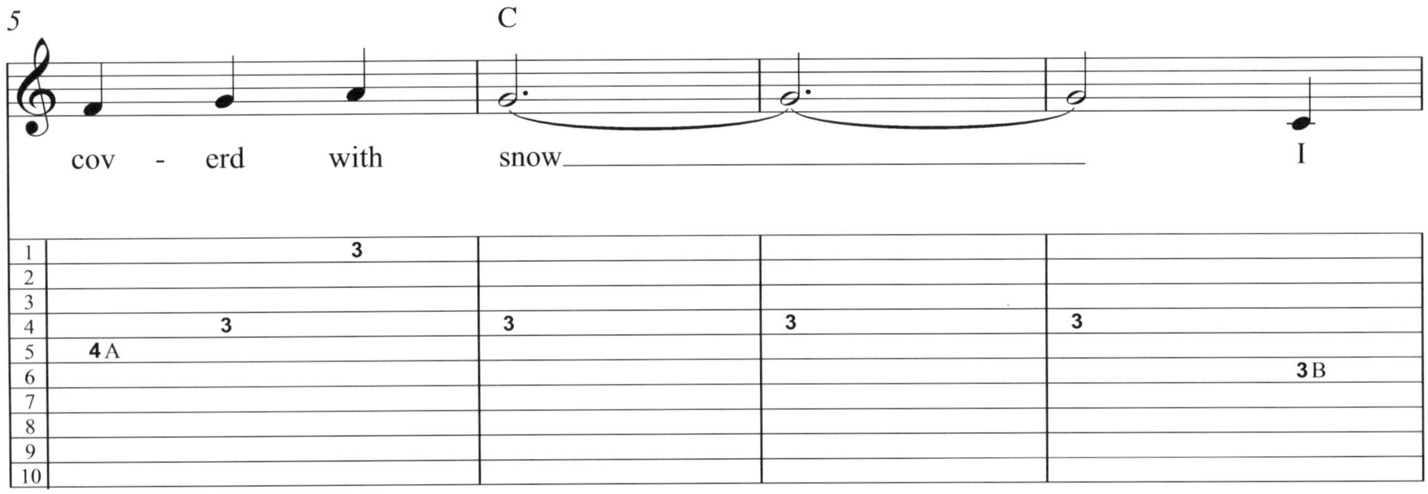

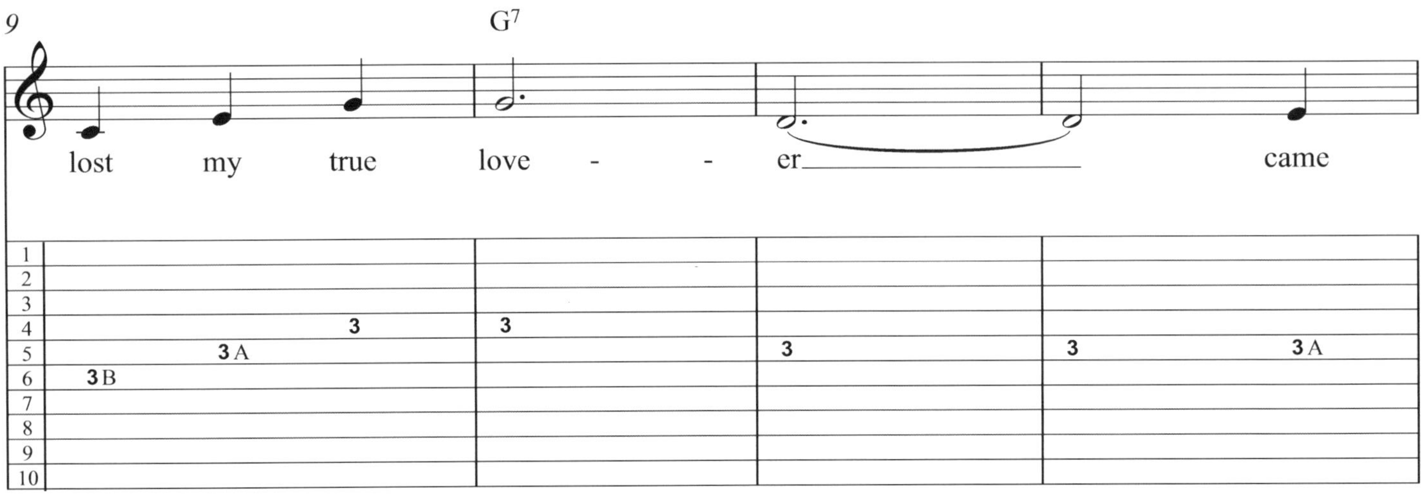

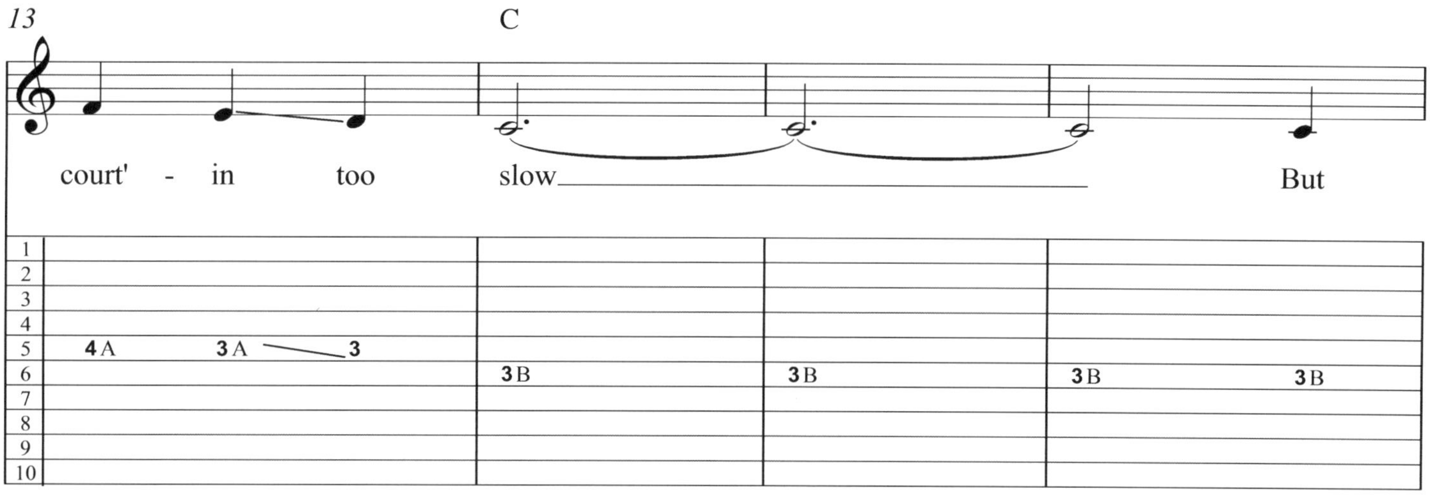

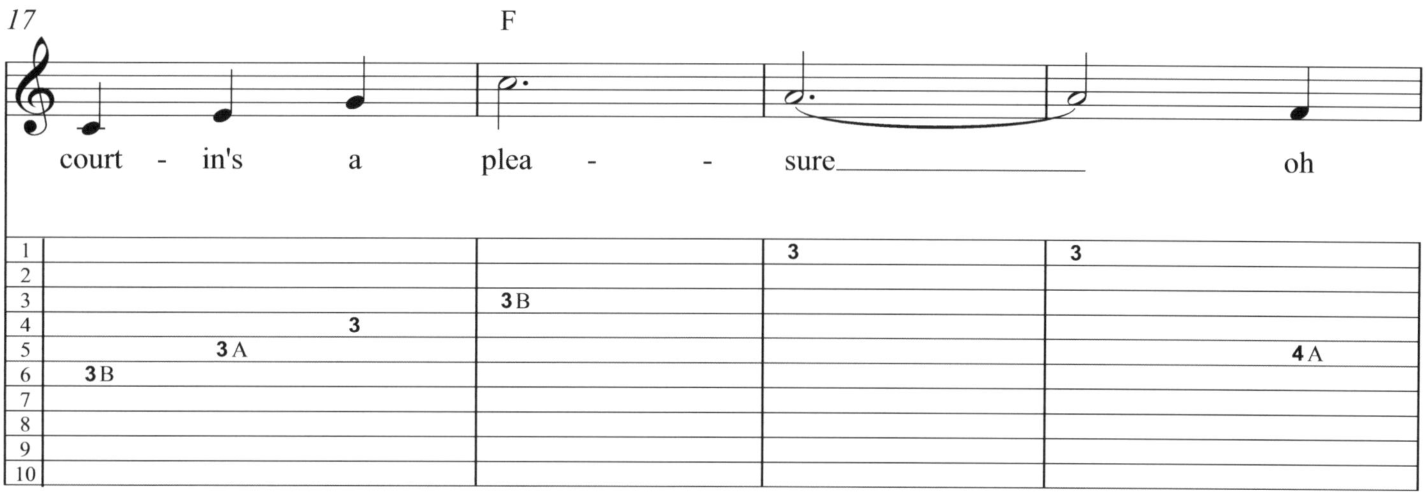

And a false hearted lover is worse than a thief
For a thief will just rob you and take all you save
But a false hearted lover will lead you to the grave
And the grave will decay you and turn you to dust

Not one girl in a hundred a poor boy can trust
They'll hug you and kiss you and tell you more lies
Than cross lines on a railroad or stars in the skies
So come all your maidens and listen to me

Never place your affections on a green willow tree
For the leaves they will wither and the roots they will die
You'll all be forsaken and never know why.

Away in a Manger

This beautiful Christmas song has been recorded by many artists including Emmylou Harris and the Louvin Brothers. It uses pedals A and B extensively.

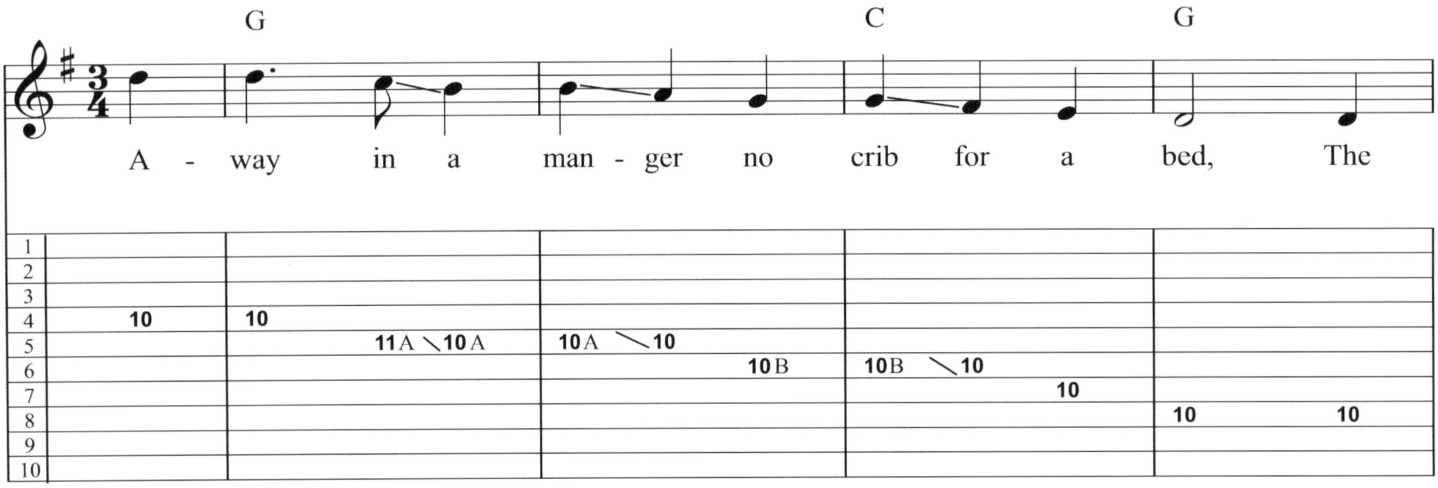

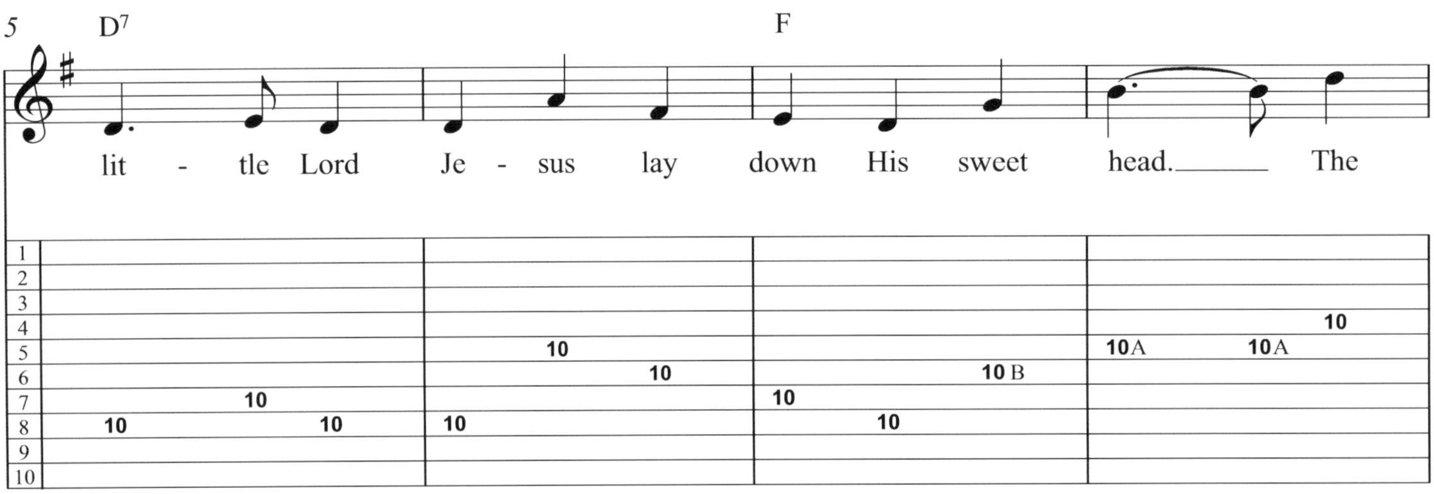

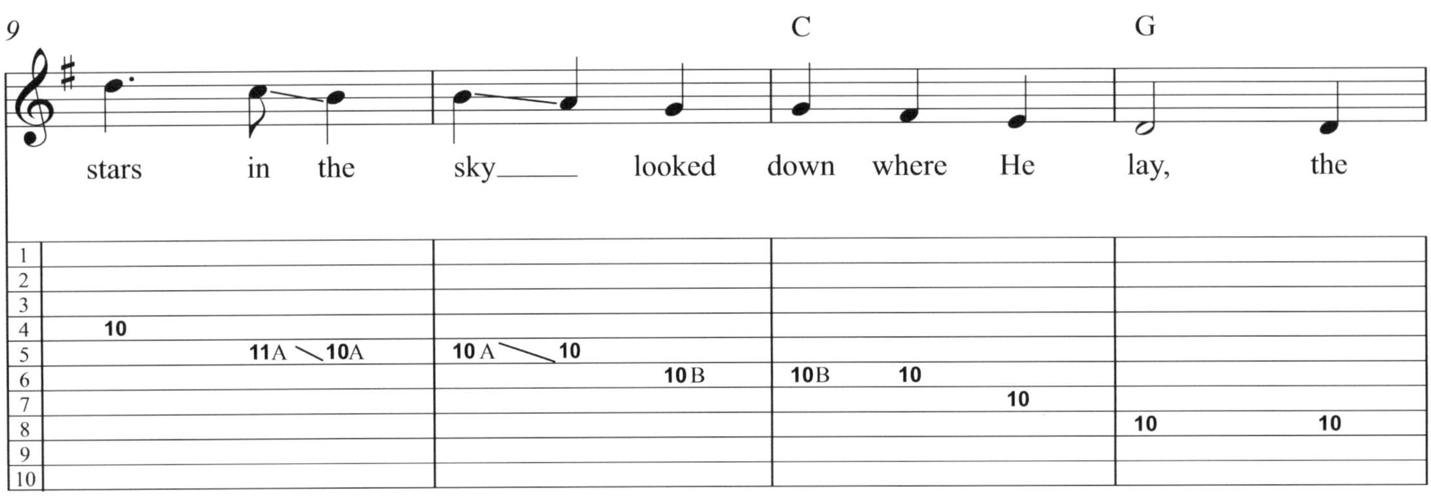

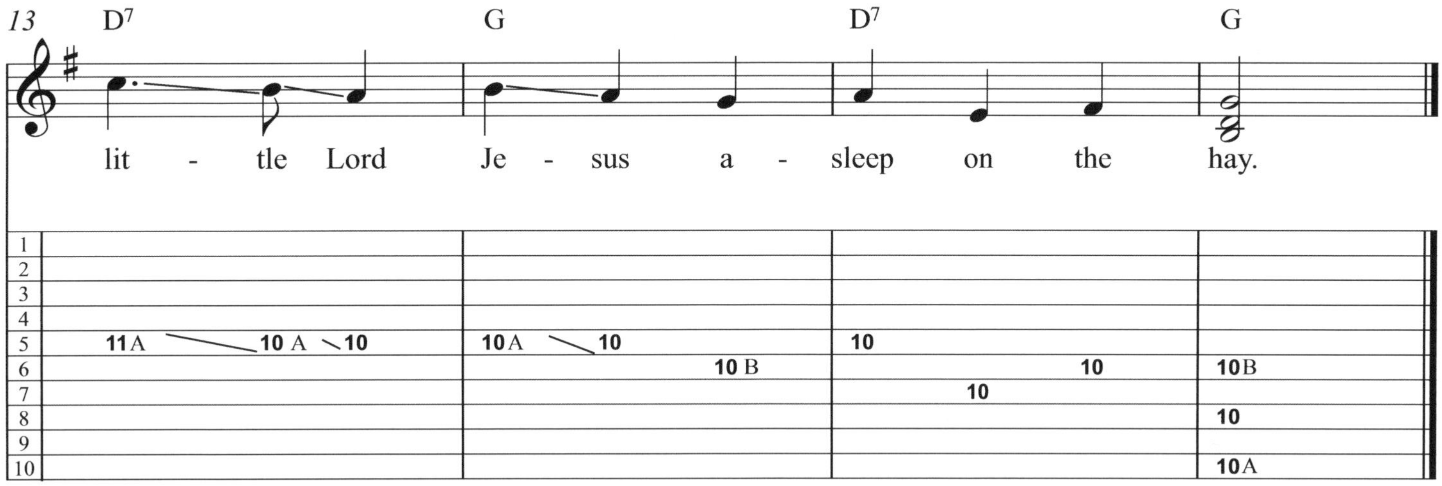

The cattle are lowing
The Baby awakes
But little Lord Jesus
No crying He makes

I love You, Lord Jesus
Look down from the sky
And stay by my side
Until morning is nigh

Be near me, Lord Jesus
I ask You to stay
Close by me forever
And love me I pray

Bless all the dear children
In Your tender care
And fit us for heaven
To live with You there

Foggy Mountain Top

Lester Flatt, Earl Scruggs, and Maybell Carter all have great arrangements of this tune.

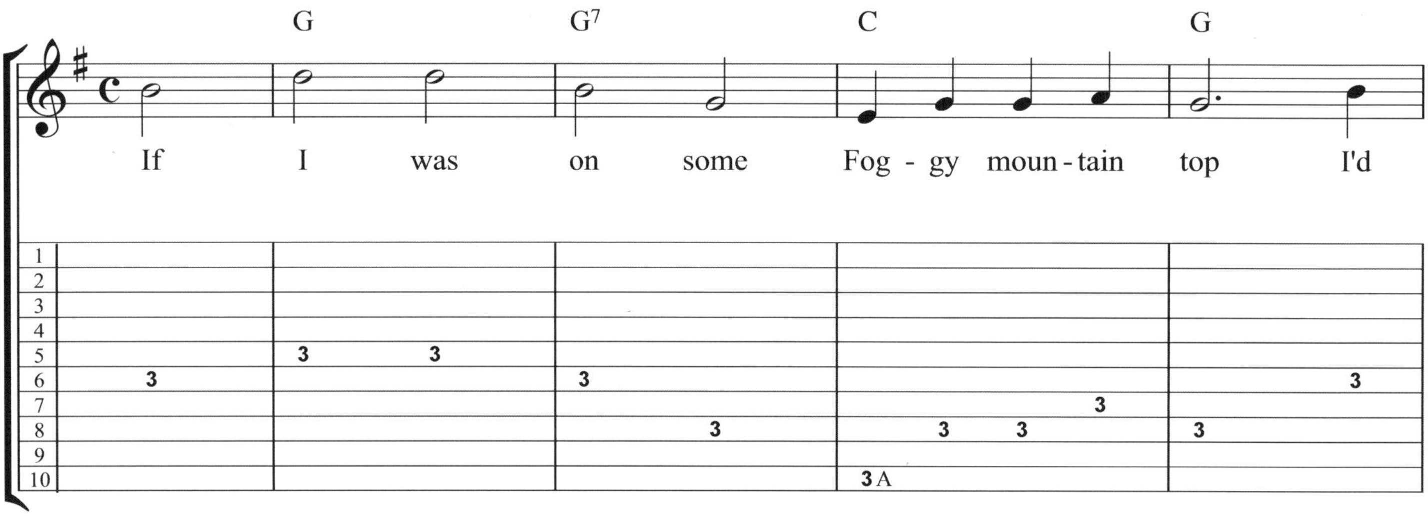

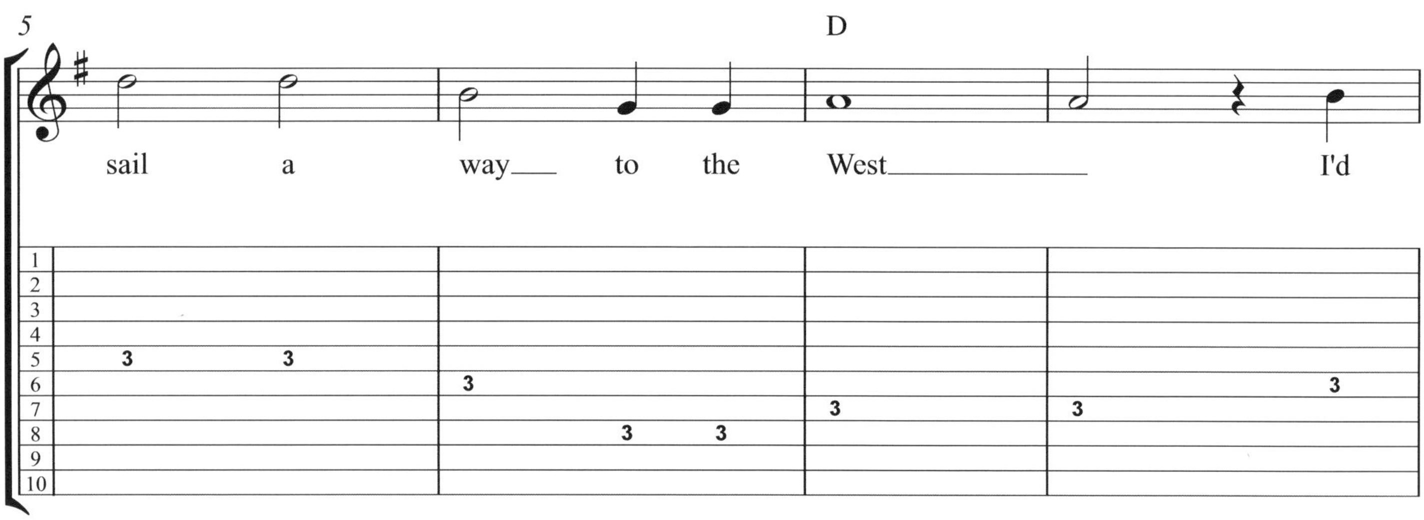

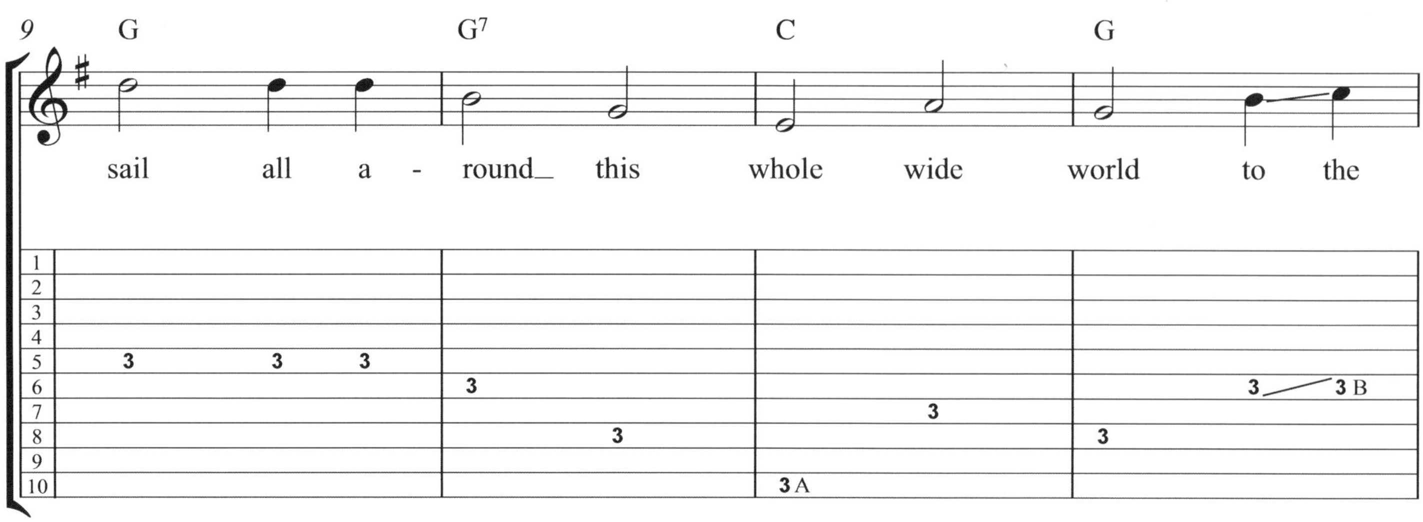

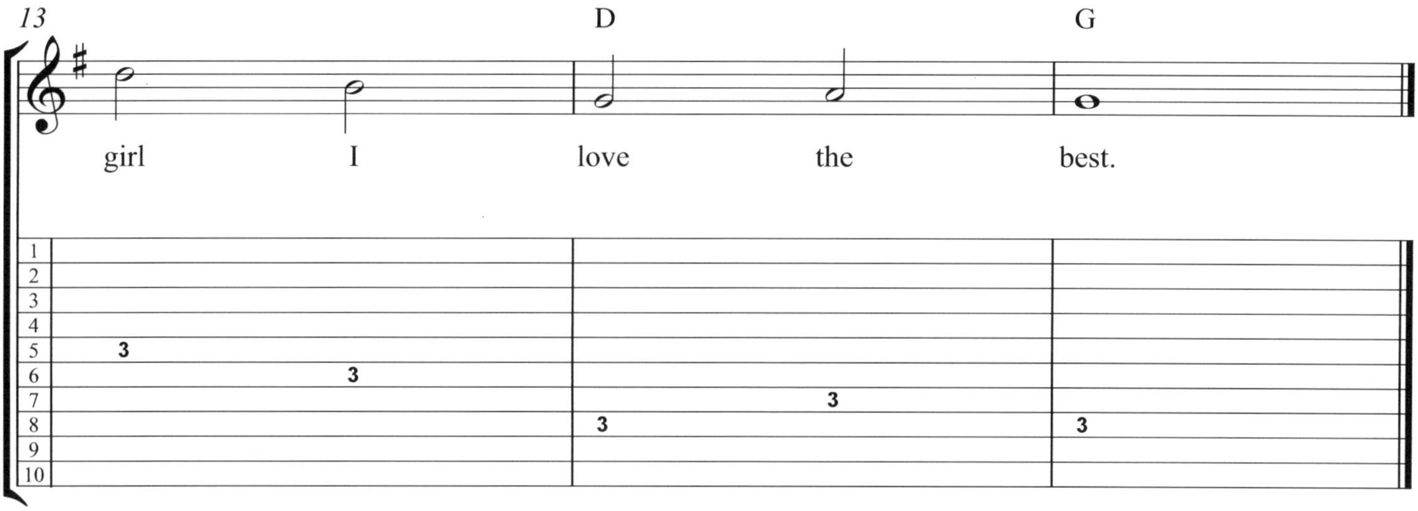

If I had listened what mama says
I would not have been here today
A-lying around this old jail house
A-weeping my sweet life away

Oh, if you see that girl of mine
There's something you must tell her
She need not be foolin' no time away
To court some other feller

Oh, she's caused me to weep, she's caused me to mourn
She caused me to leave my home
For the lonesome pine and the good old times
I'm on my way back home

Oh, when you go a-courtin'
I'll tell you how to do
Pull off that long-tailed roustabout
Put on your navy blue

Buffalo Gals

"Buffalo Gals" is an American folksong that has been recorded by many artists, including Grandpa Jones, Arlo Guthrie and the great banjo artist, Alan Munde. In measure 2, pick only 8A and then slowly release the A pedal.

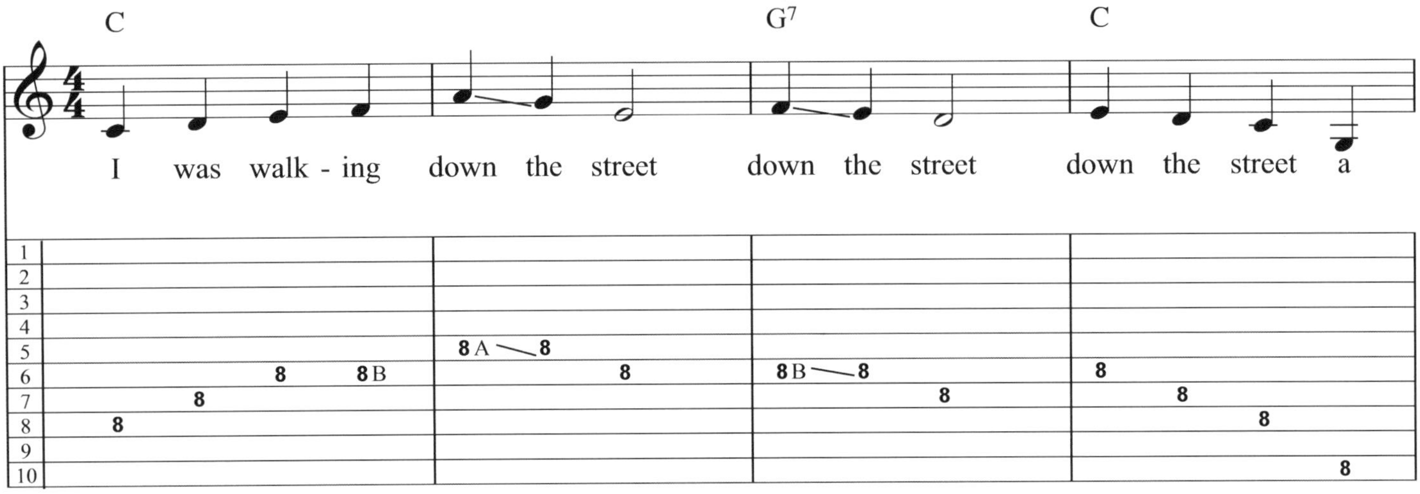

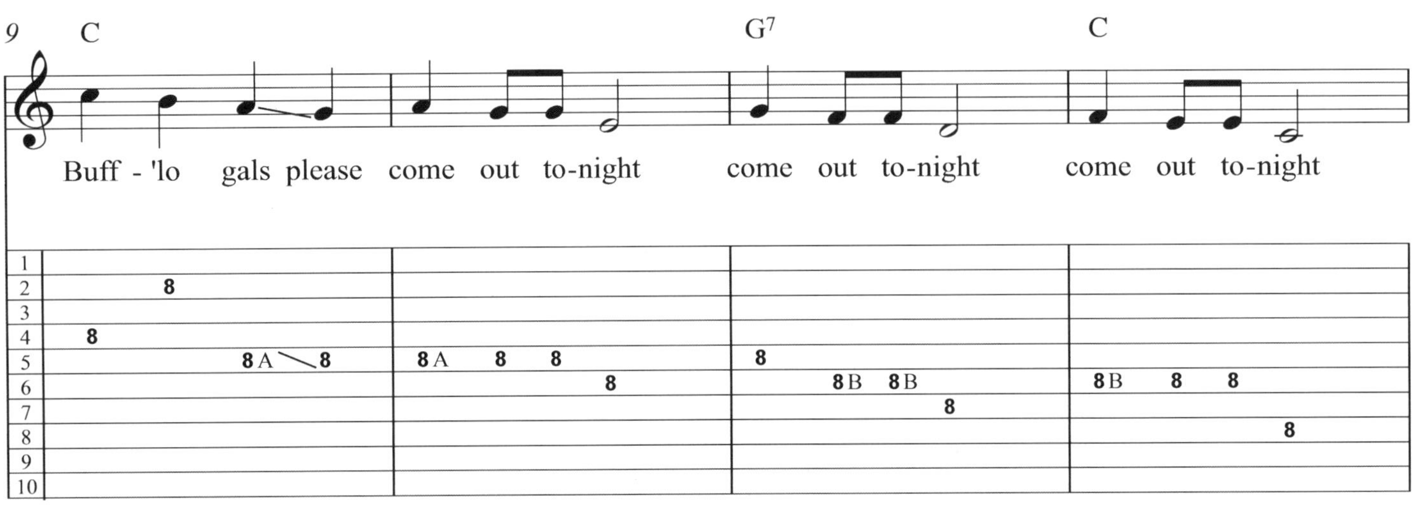

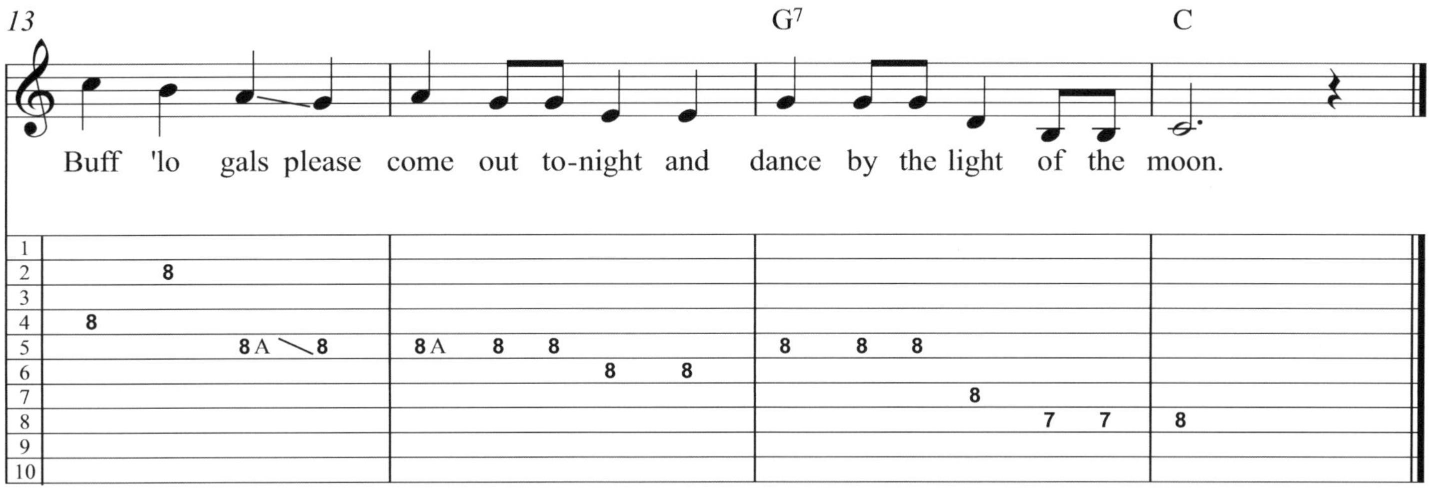

As I was walking down the street,
Down the street, down the street,
A pretty little gal I chanced to meet,
Oh, she was fair to see.

I stopped her and we had a talk,
Had a talk, had a talk,
Her feet took up the whole sidewalk
And left no room for me.

I asked her if she'd have a dance,
Have a dance, have a dance,
I thought that I might have a chance
To shake a foot with her.

I danced with a gal with a hole in her stockin',
And her heel kept a-knockin', and her toes kept a-rockin'
I danced with a gal with a hole in her stockin'
And we danced by the light of the moon.

Careless Love

I first heard this song sung by June Carter, the wife of Johnny Cash. I consider it a country music staple.

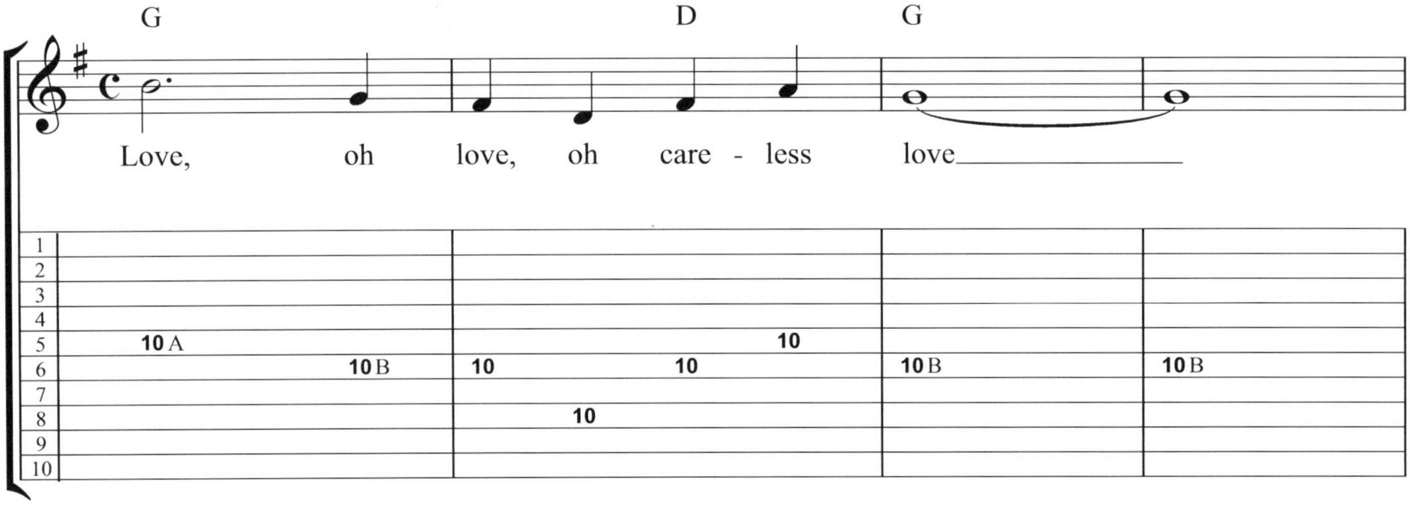

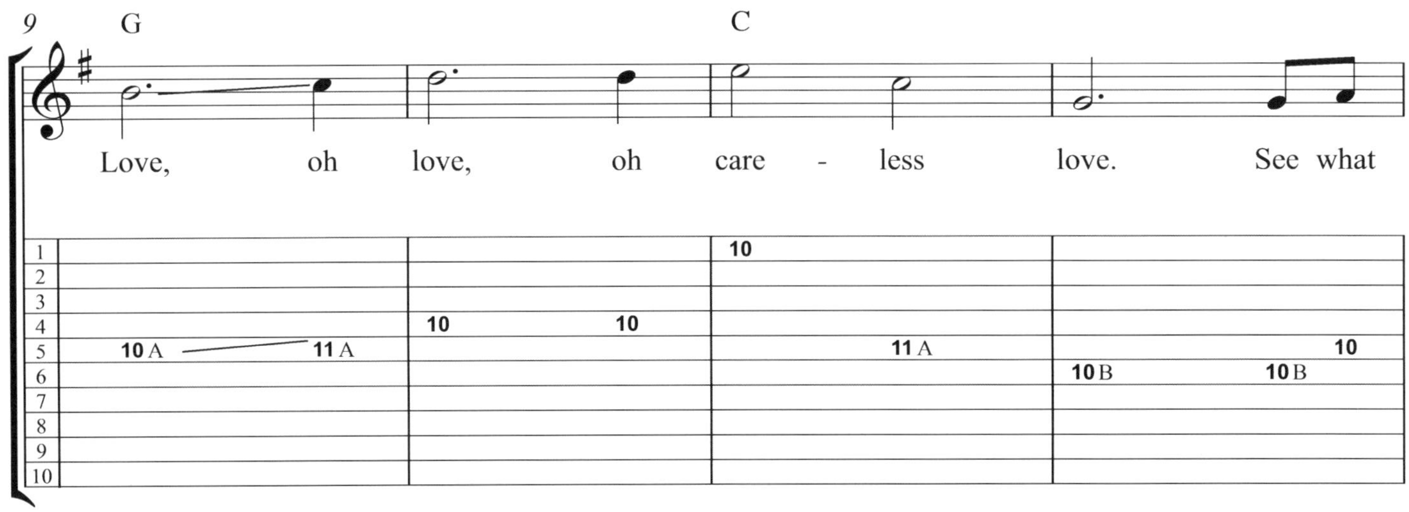

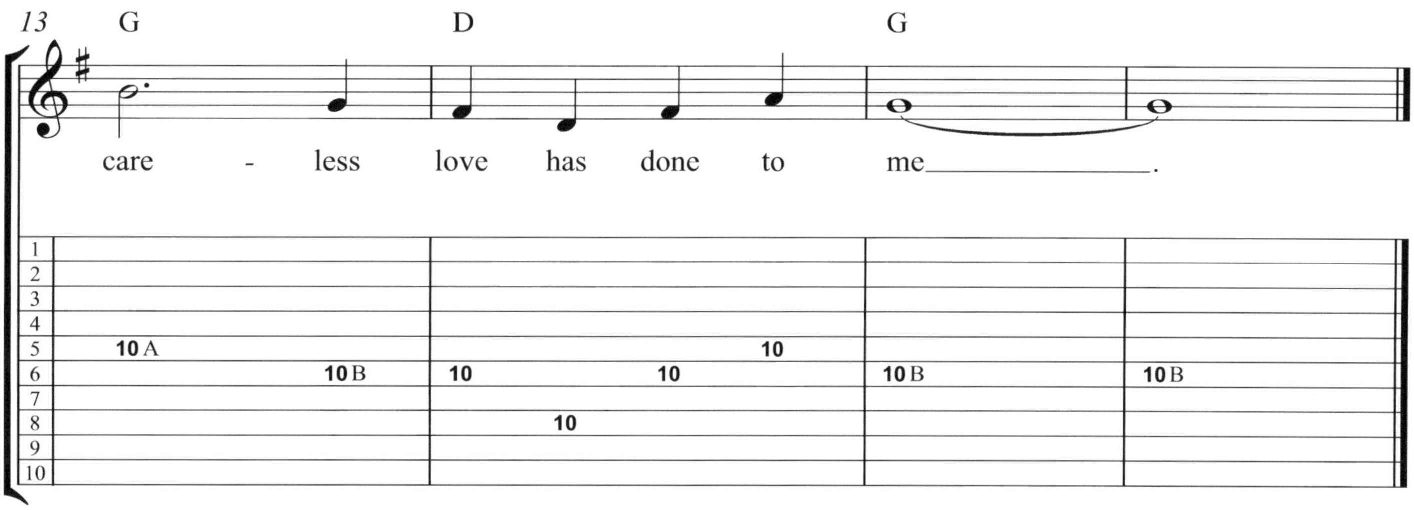

Love, oh love, oh careless love
In your clutches of desire
You've made me break a many true vow
Then you set my very soul on fire

Love, oh love, oh careless love
All my happiness bereft
You've filled my heart with weary old blues
Now I'm walkin', talkin' to myself

Love, oh love, oh careless love
Trusted you now, it's too late
You've made me throw my old friend down
That's why I sing this song of hate

Love, oh love, oh careless love
Night and day, I weep and moan
You brought the wrong man into this life of mine
For my sins, till judgment I'll atone

Wildwood Flower

This is an important song in the history of country music. It was written by A. P. Carter of the famous Carter family.

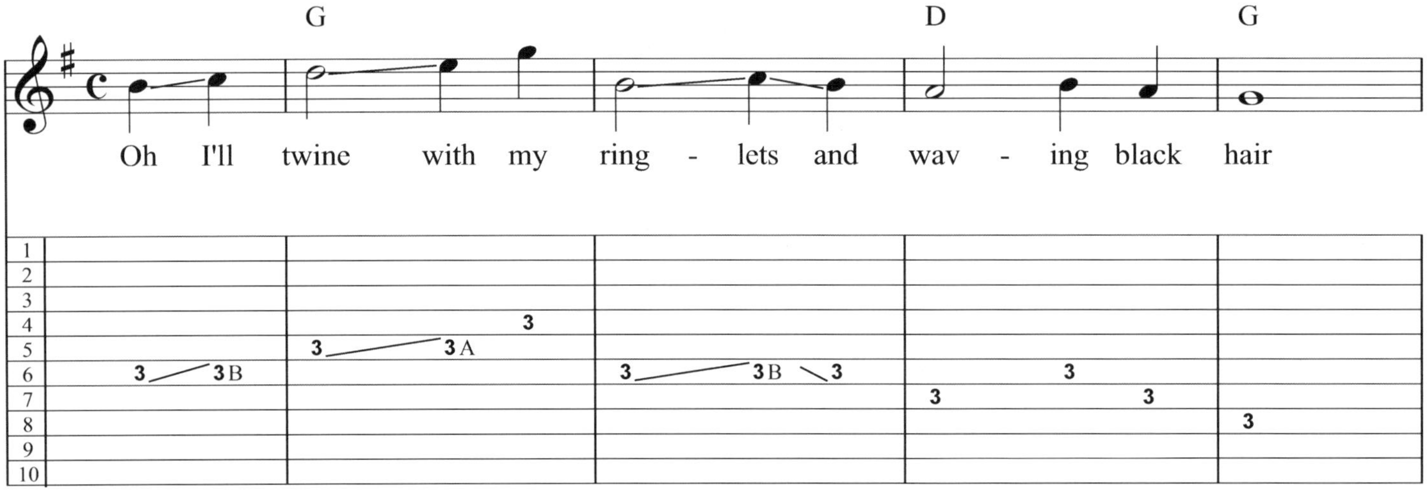

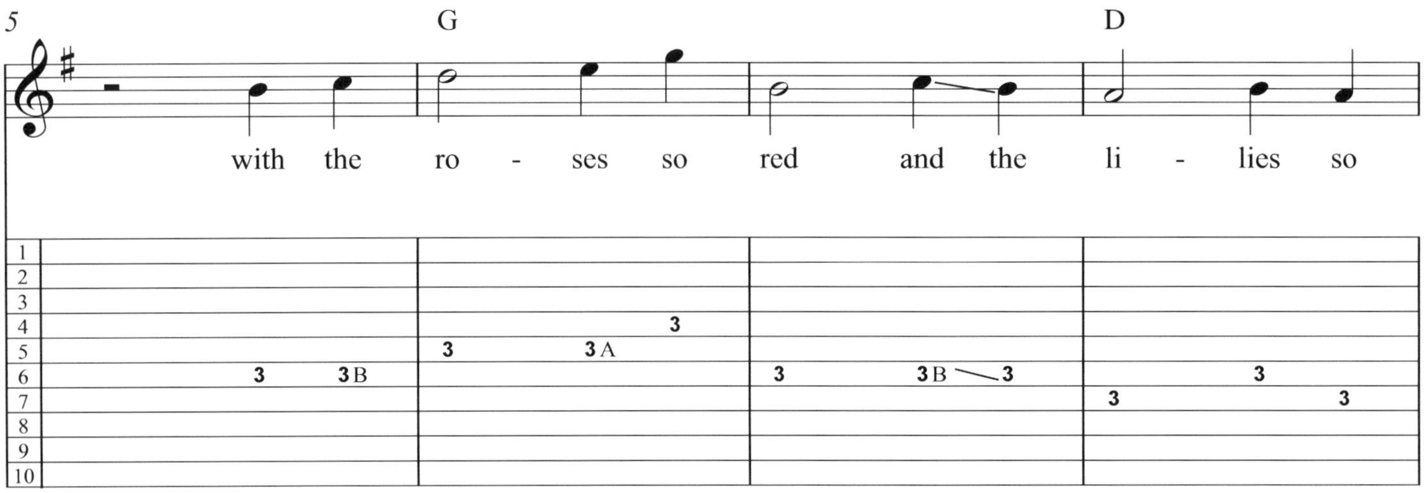

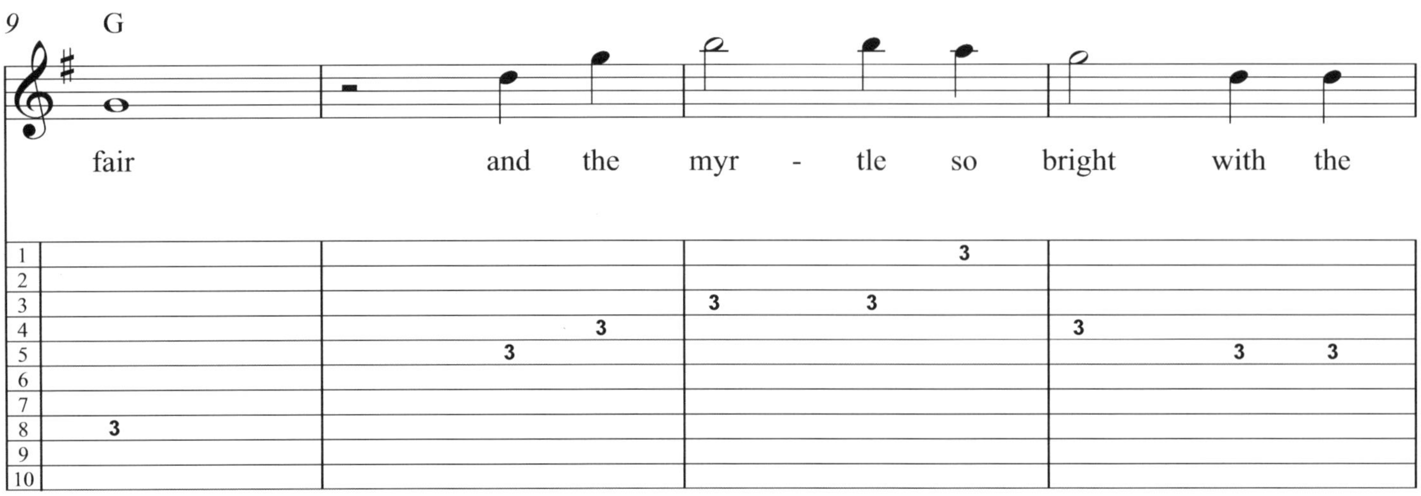

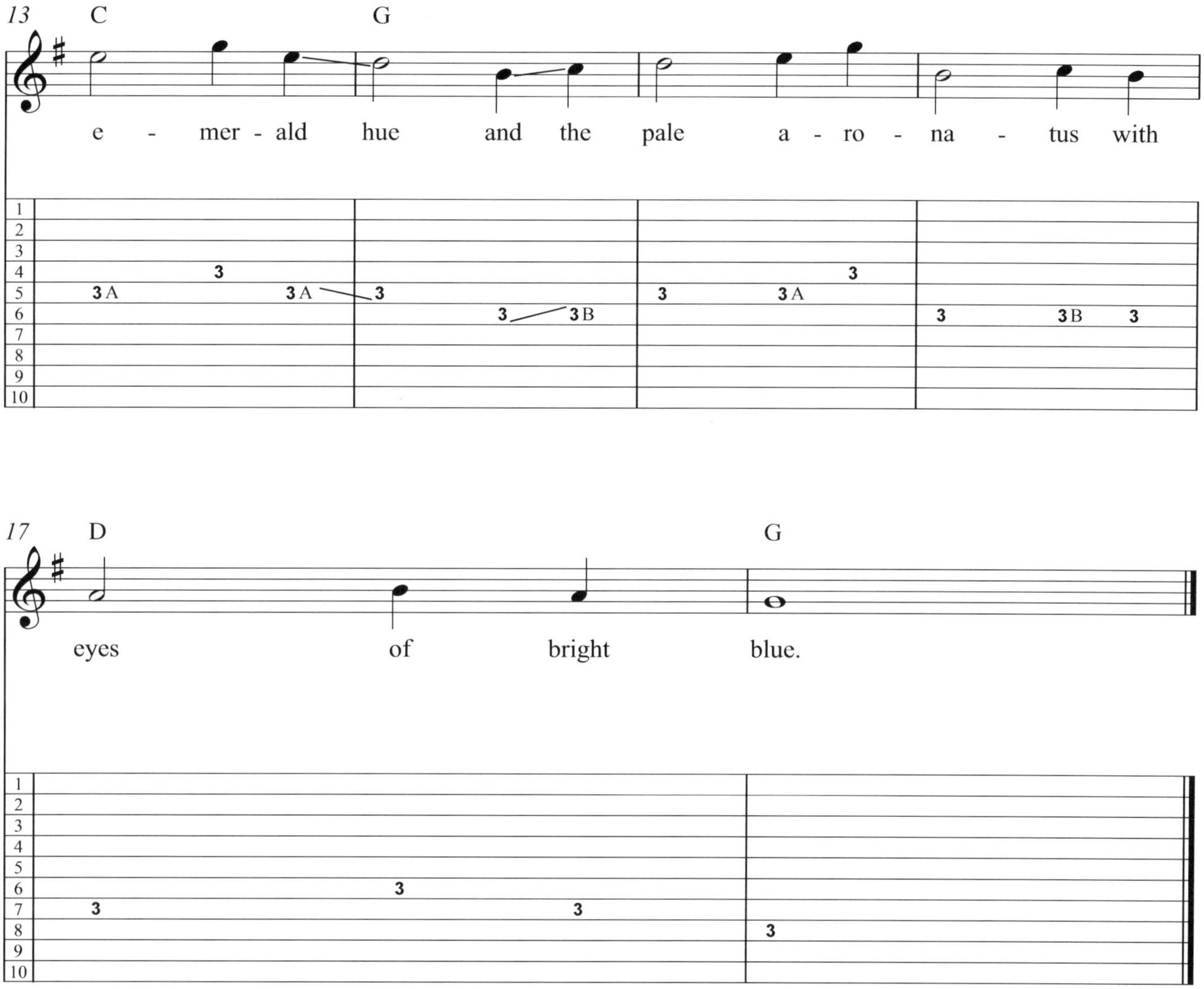

I will dance, I will sing and my laugh shall be gay
I will charm every heart, in his crown I will sway
When I awoke from my dreaming my idol was clay
All portion of love had all flown away

Oh, he taught me to love him and promised to love
And to cherish me over all others above
How my heart is now wondering no misery can tell
He's left with no warning, no word of farewell

Oh, he taught me to love him and called me his flower
That was blooming to cheer him through life's dreary hour
Oh, I long to see him and regret the dark hour
He's one that neglected this pale wildwood flower

10

The Blue-Tail Fly

The Andrews Sisters, Burl Ives, and Lead Belly recorded the 1840's minstrel song "The Blue-Tail Fly".

And when he would ride in the afternoon
I'd follow after, with a hickory broom
The pony being rather shy
When bitten by blue-tail fly

One day, he ride around the farm
The flies so numerous, they did swarm
One chanced to bite him on the thigh
The devil take the blue-tail fly

The pony run, he jumped, he pitch
He threw my friend in the ditch
He died and the jury wondered why
The verdict was the blue-tail fly

They lay him under a 'simmon tree
His epitaph is there to see
"Beneath this stone, I'm forced to lie
Victim of the blue-tail fly"

11

The Unclouded Day

This great gospel tune has been performed by Johnny Cash, Willie Nelson, Toby Keith and many other artists.

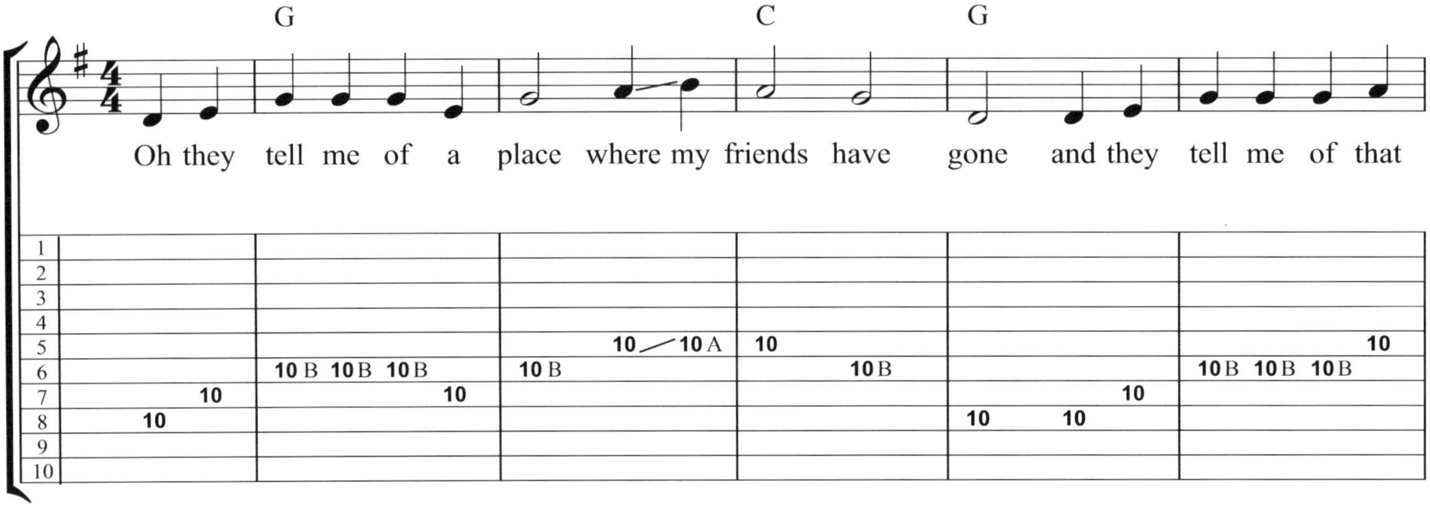

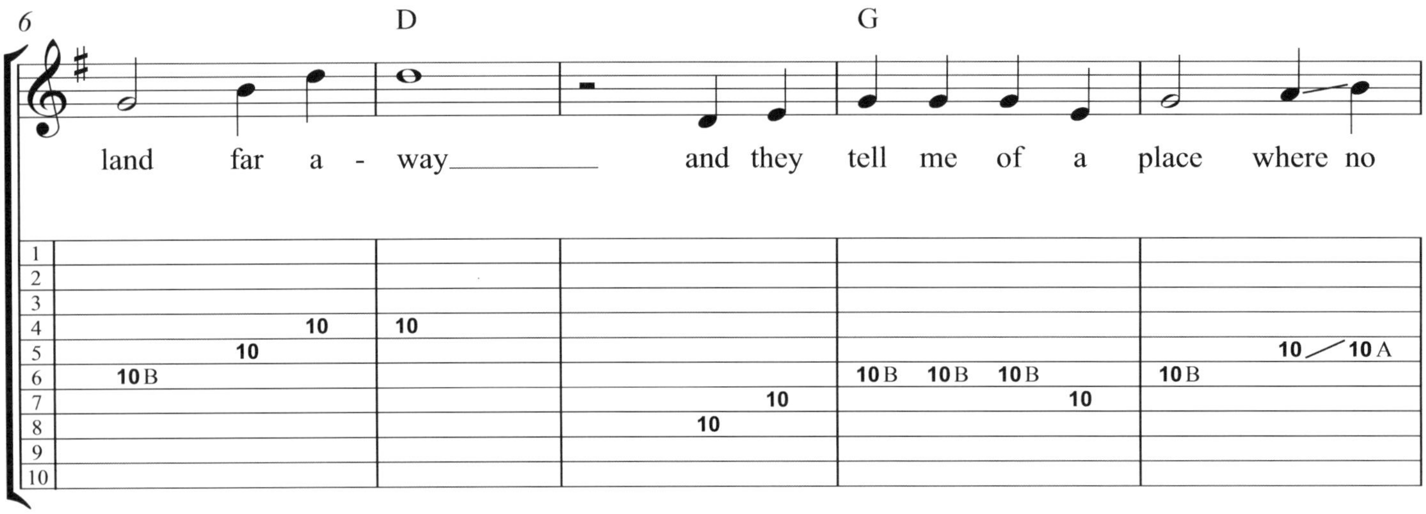

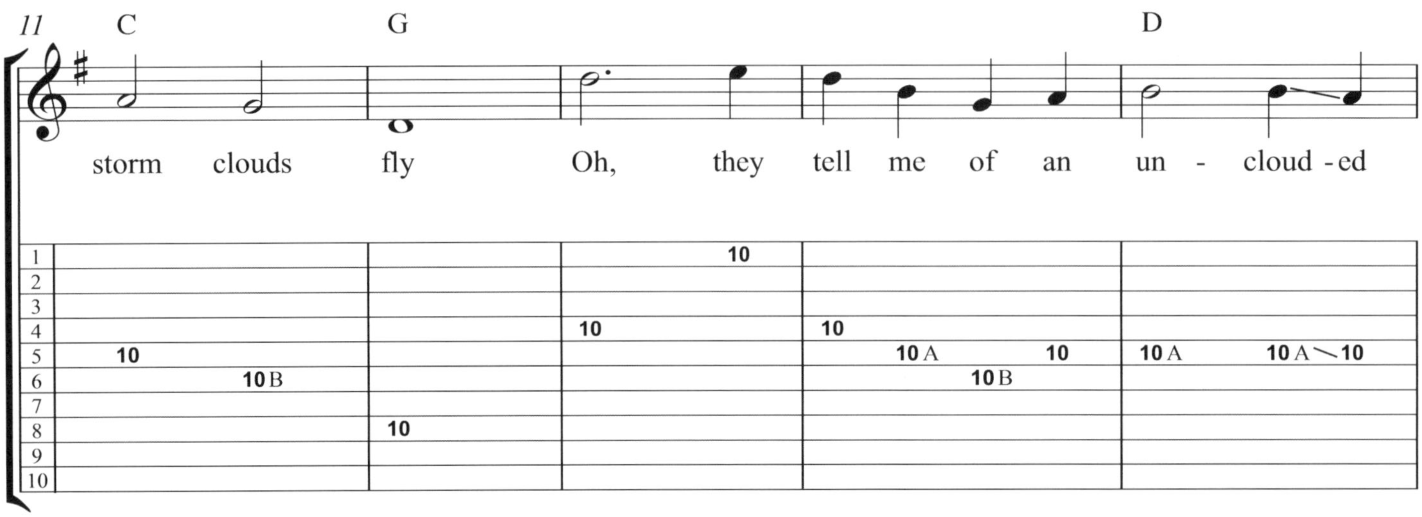

16 G G
day Oh the land of a cloud - less day
21 D
Oh the land of an un - cloud - ed sky Oh they
26 G C G
tell me of a place where my friends have gone Oh they

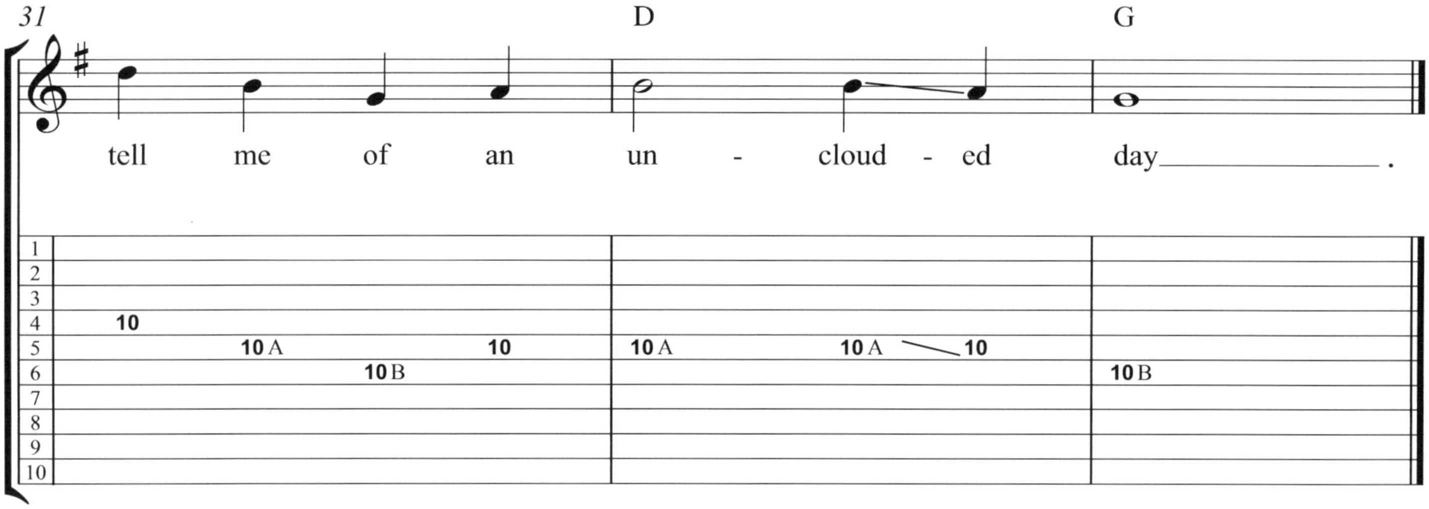

Oh, they tell me of a King in His beauty there
And they tell me that mine eyes shall behold
Where He sits on the throne that is whiter than snow
In the city that is made of gold

And His smile drives their sorrows all away
And they tell me that no tears ever come again
In that lovely land of unclouded day

Oh! Susanna

"Oh! Susanna" is one of the most popular American songs ever written. It has been recorded by the Byrds, Gene Autry, John McEuen, and many others. Here, we have added harmony notes for the first time in this book.

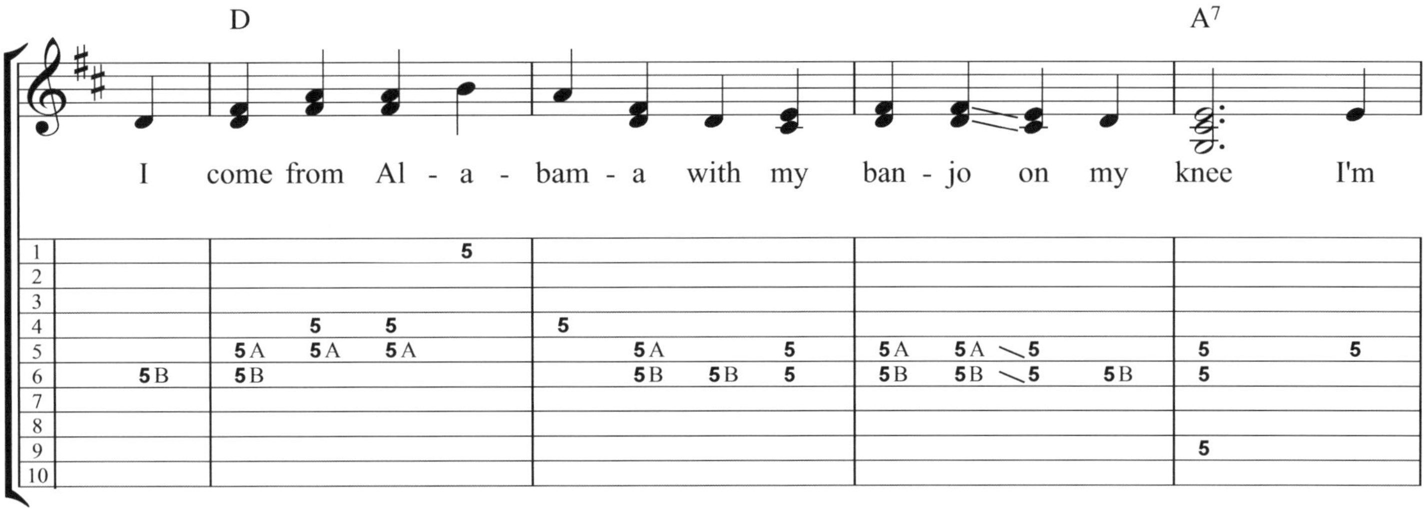

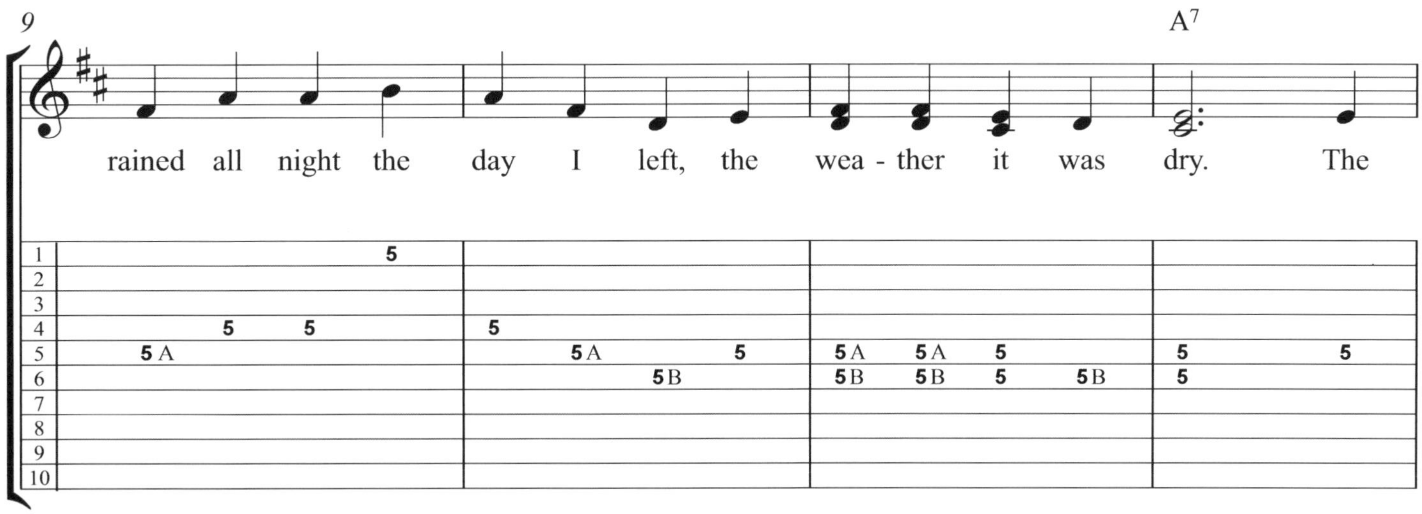

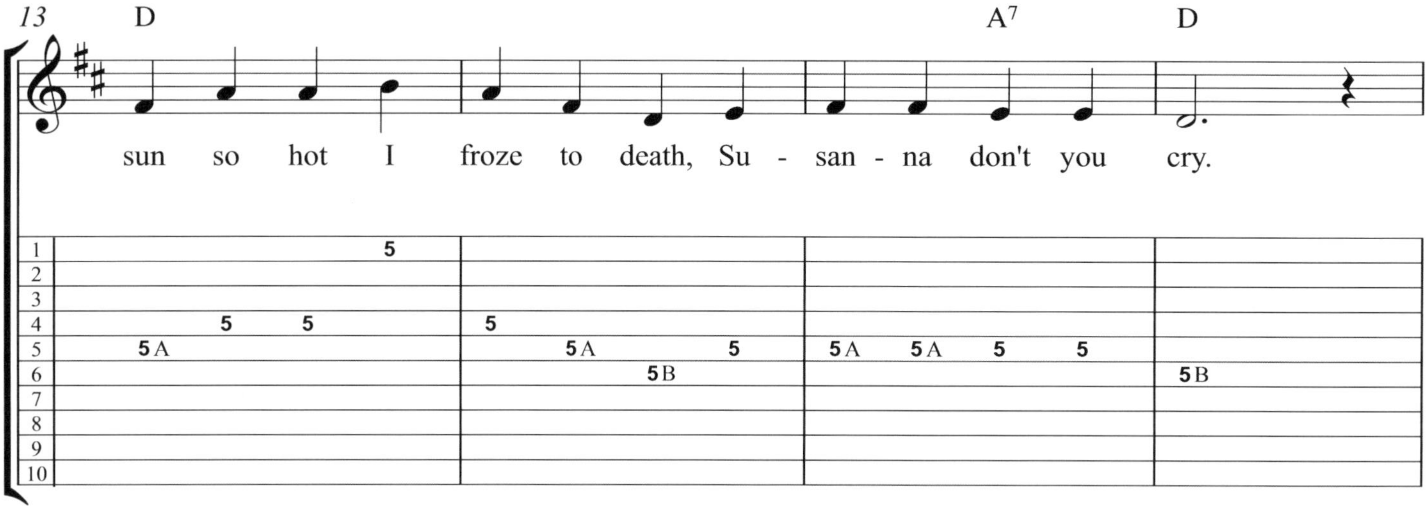
13
D
A7
D
sun so hot I froze to death, Su - san - na don't you cry.

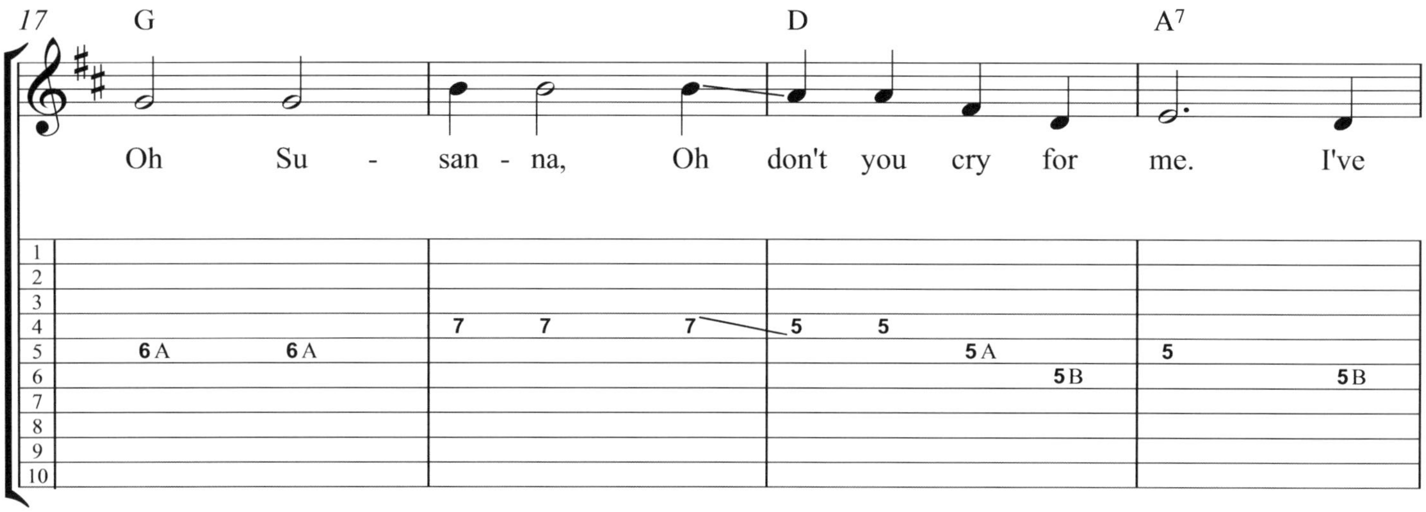
17
G
D
A7
Oh Su - san - na, Oh don't you cry for me. I've

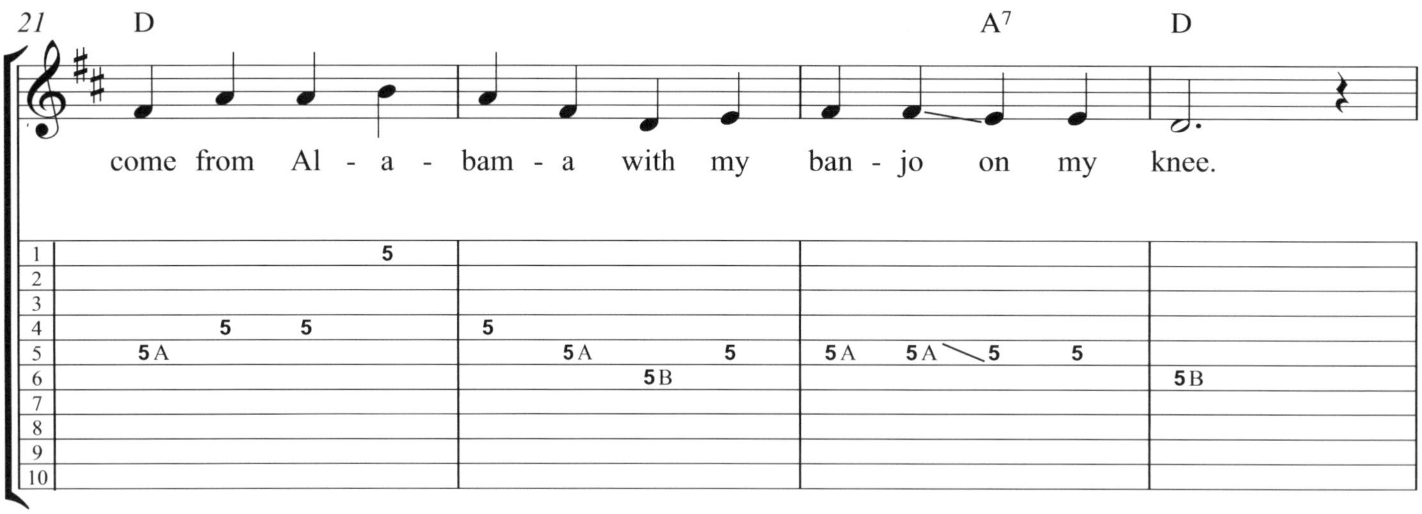
21
D
A7
D
come from Al - a - bam - a with my ban - jo on my knee.

Had a dream the other night when everything was still,
I thought I saw Susanna coming up the hill,
A wheat cake was in her mouth, a tear was in her eye,
I said I'm coming from the south, Susanna don't you cry.

I soon will be in New Orleans and then I'll look around
And when I find my Susanna, I'll fall upon the ground
But if I do not find her, this man will surely die
And when I'm dead and buried, Susanna don't you cry.

13

Amazing Grace

"Amazing Grace" has such a beautiful melody, it has become a staple of country music. A lot of great country crooners like Alan Jackson and Randy Travis have sung this tune and there are several instrumental versions. Notice the simultaneous use of the A and B pedals.

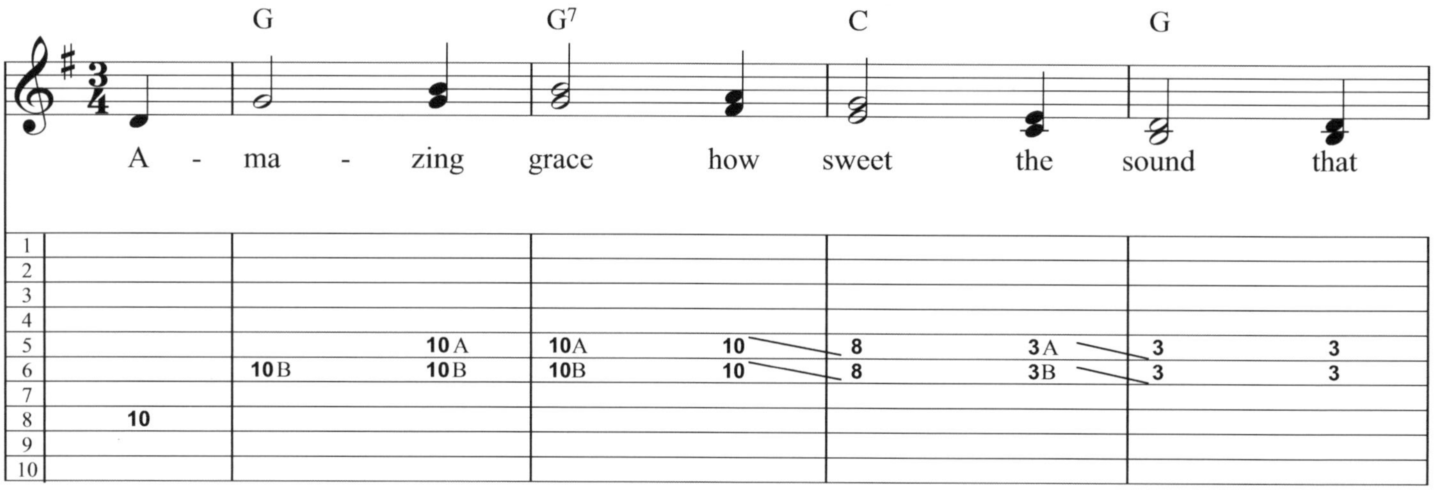

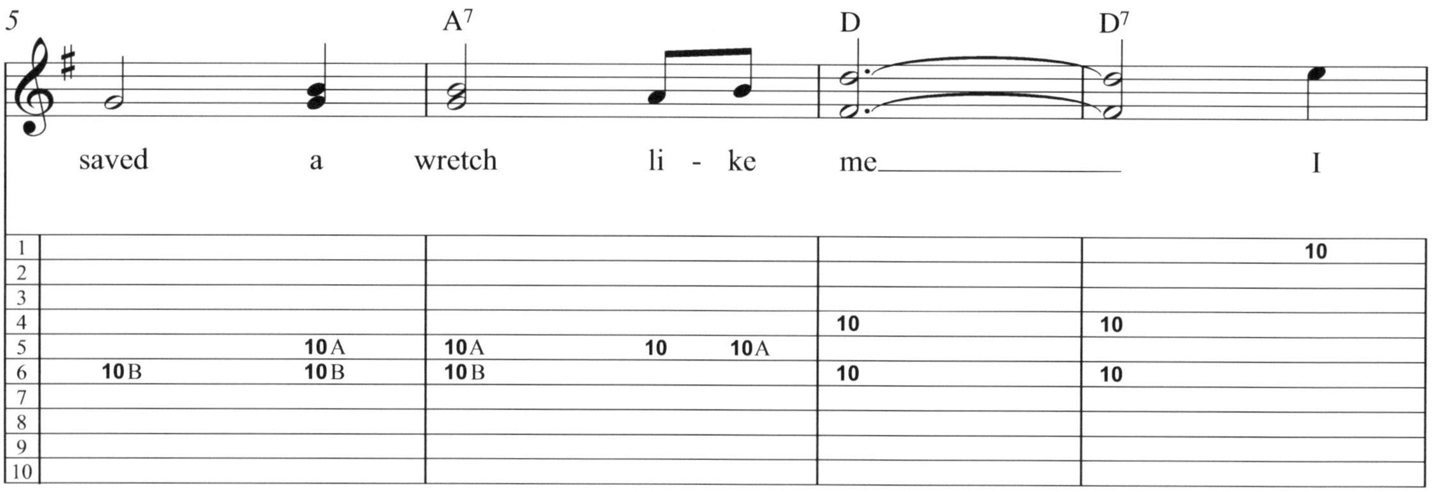

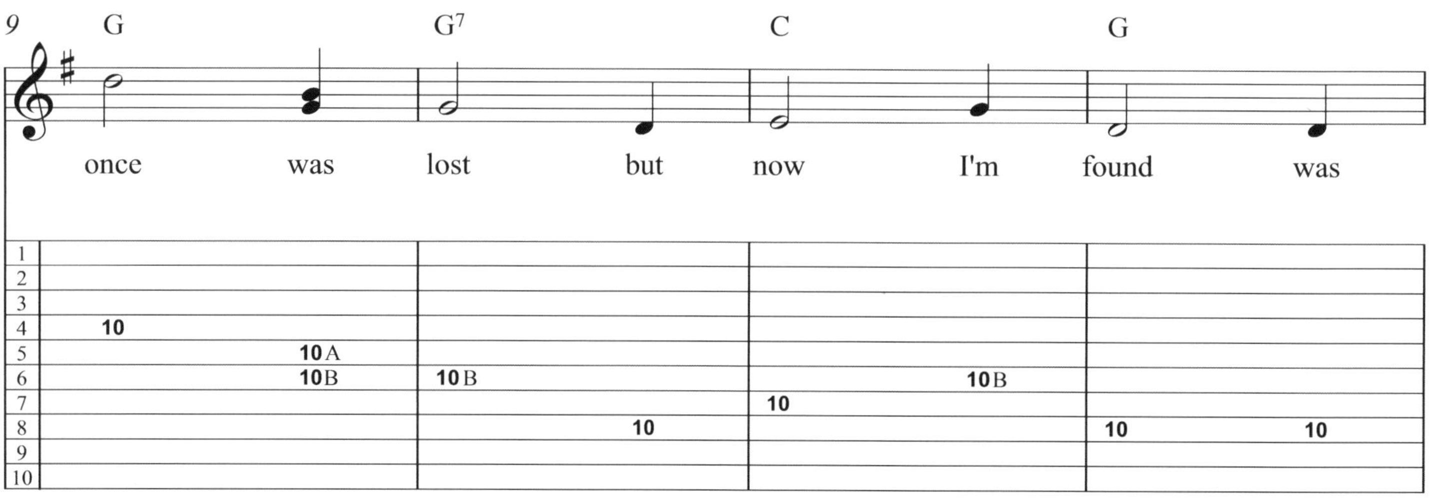

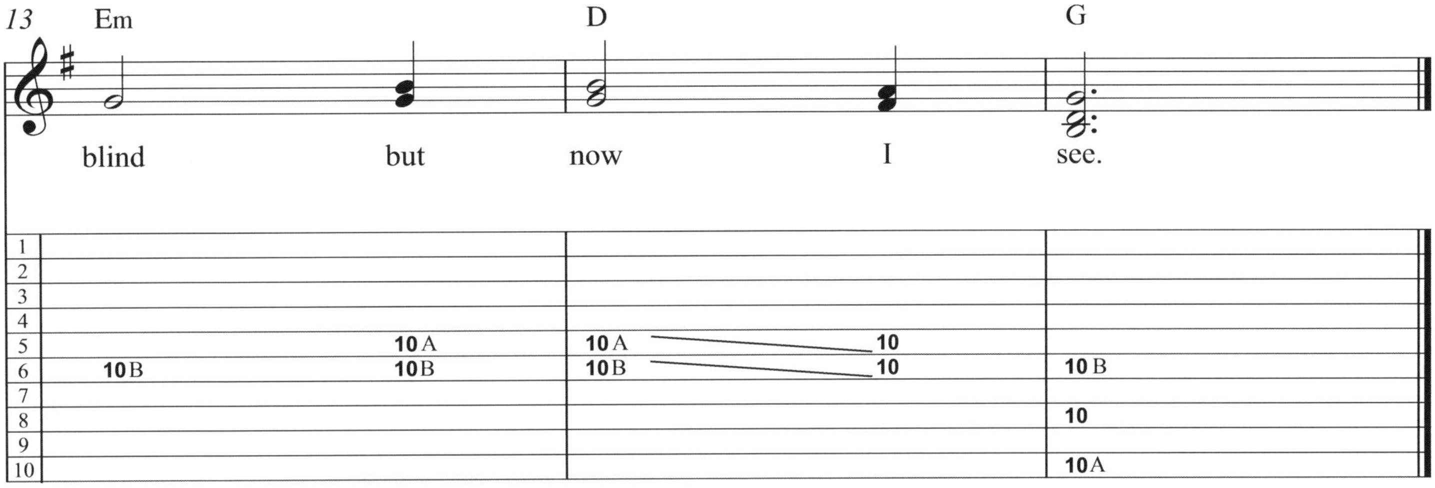

Was Grace that taught my heart to fear
And Grace, my fears relieved
How precious did that Grace appear
The hour I first believed

Through many dangers, toils and snares
We have already come
T'was Grace that brought us safe thus far
And Grace will lead us home

Amazing Grace, how sweet the sound
That saved a wretch like me
I once was lost but now am found
Was blind, but now I see

14

Jesus Loves Me

"Jesus Loves Me" is a beautiful Christian hymn that has been recorded by many artists including Whitney Houston, and Joey and Rory. This arrangement harmonizes all but the last two measures.

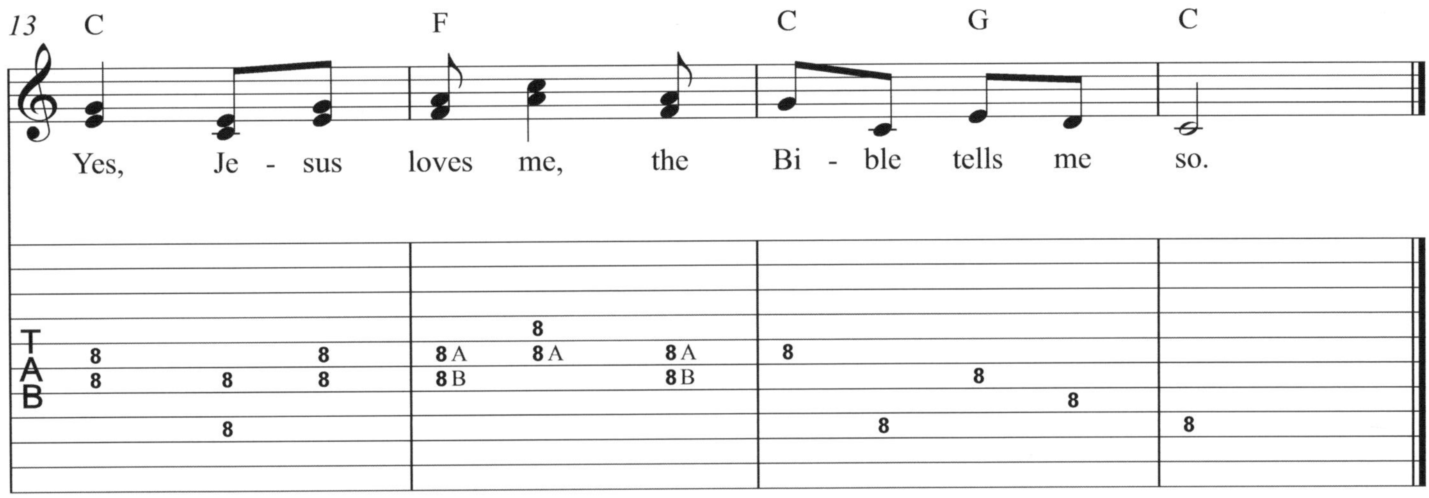

Jesus loves me! This I know,
As He loved so long ago,
Taking children on His knee,
Saying, "Let them come to Me."

Jesus loves me still today,
Walking with me on my way,
Wanting as a friend to give
Light and love to all who live.

Jesus loves me! He who died
Heaven's gate to open wide;
He will wash away my sin,
Let His little child come in.

Jesus loves me! He will stay
Close beside me all the way;
Thou hast bled and died for me,
I will henceforth live for Thee.

15

Goodnight, Ladies

"Goodnight, Ladies" is a famous song from the musical *The Music Man*. It was also the closing song of *the Lawrence Welk Show.*

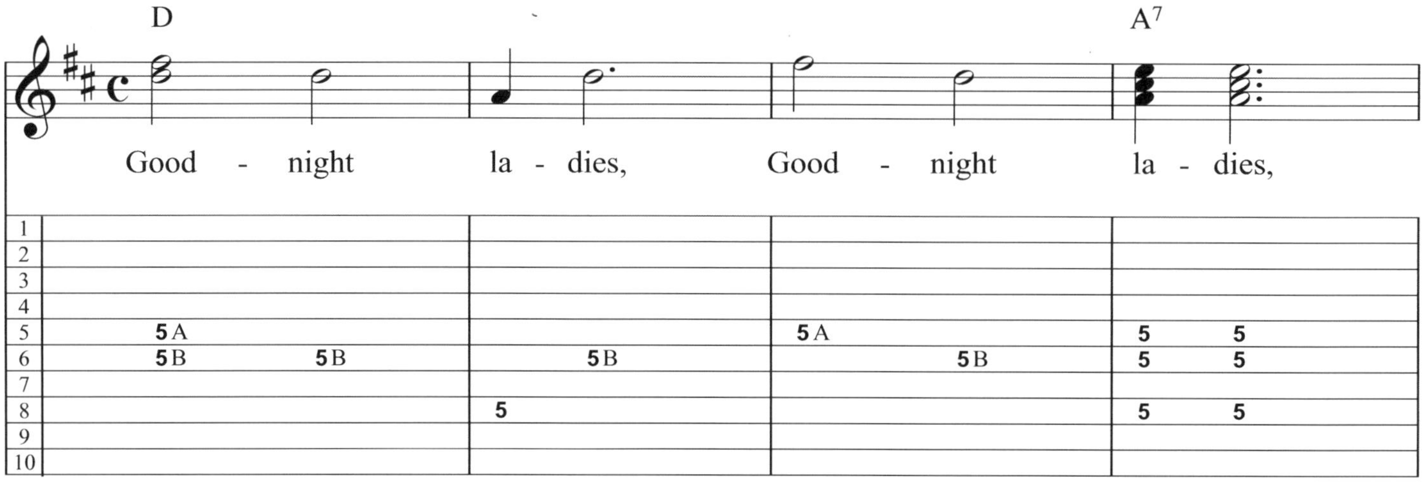

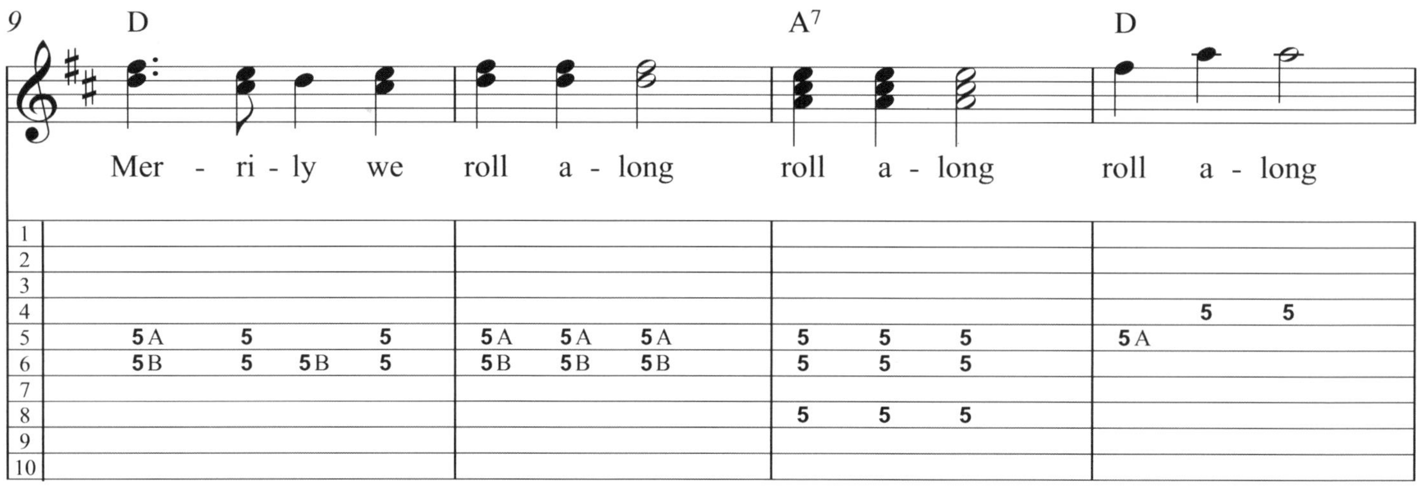

13
D
A7
D
Mer - ri - ly we roll a - long O'er the dark blue seas.
17
G
A7
Fare - well la - dies Fare - well la - dies,
21
D
D7
G
D
A7
D
fare - well la - dies, we're goin' to leave you now.

16

Banks of the Ohio

Many great bluegrass artists, including Tony Rice, Bill Monroe and The Country Gentleman have sung this love song.

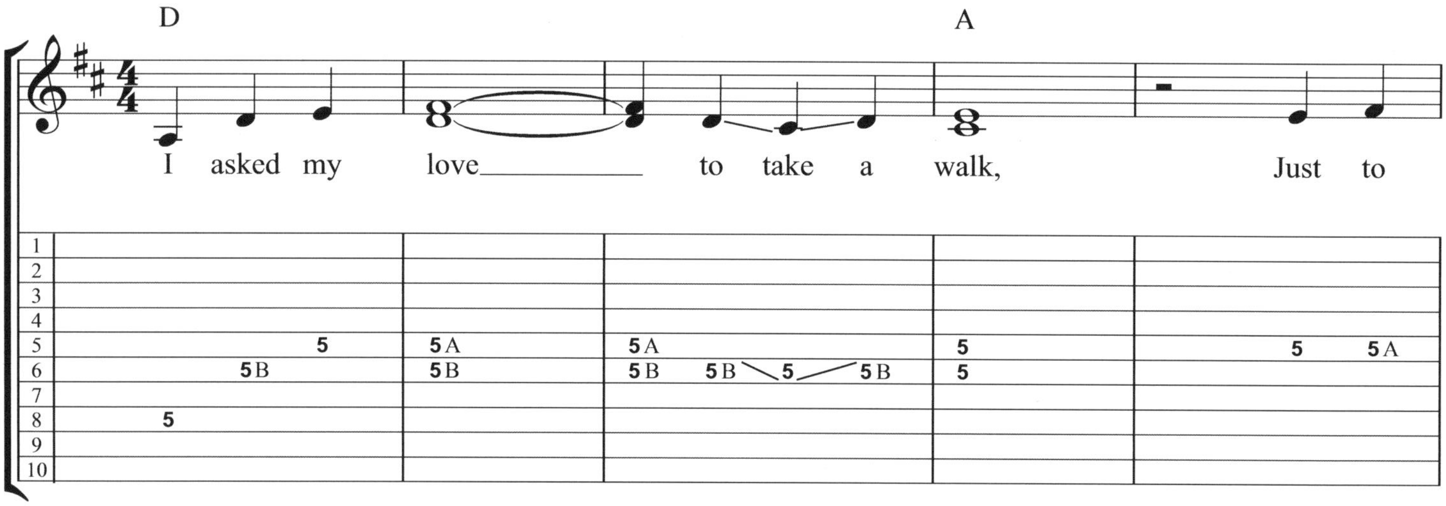

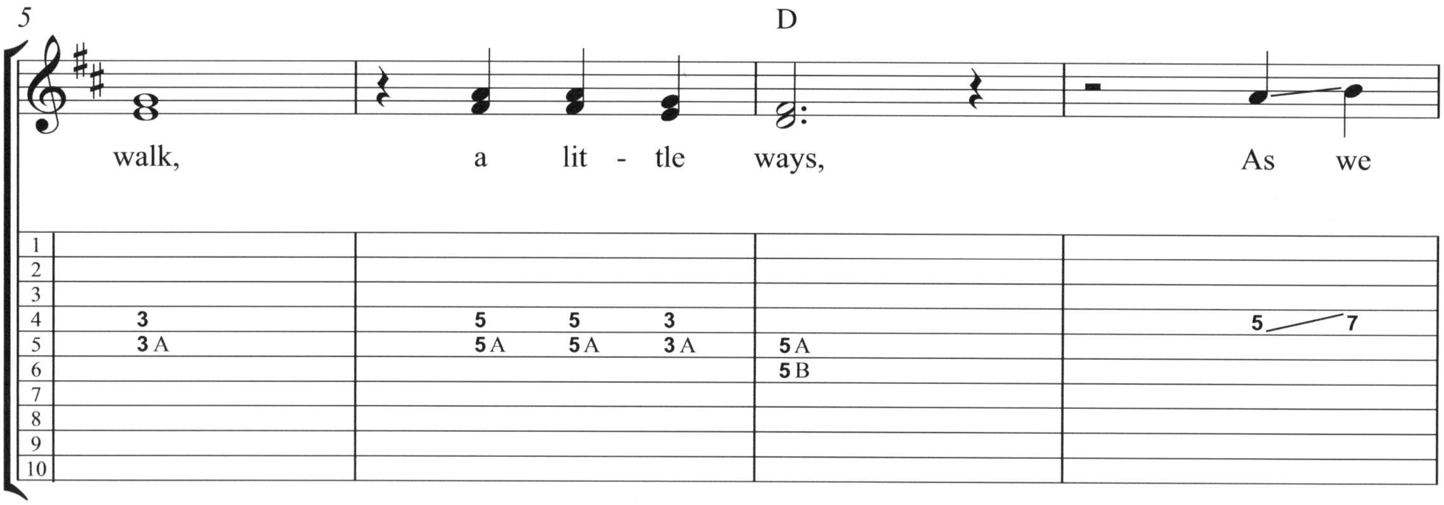

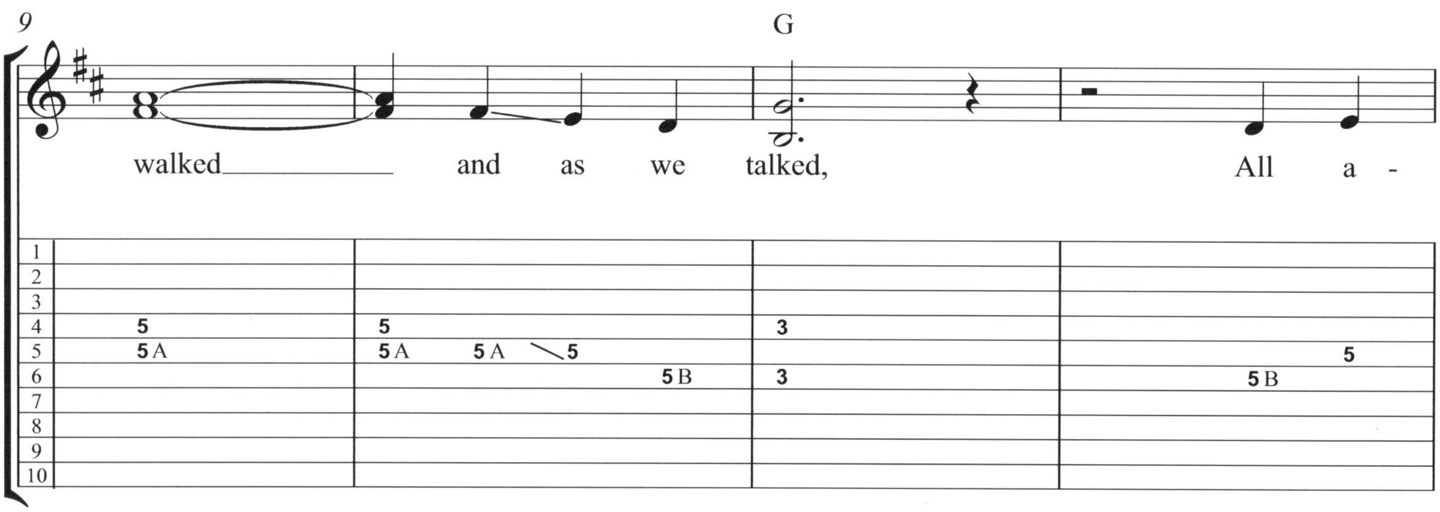

13
D A D
bout our wed - ding day. On - ly
17
A
say that you'll be mine, In our
21
D
home we'll hap - py be. Down be - side

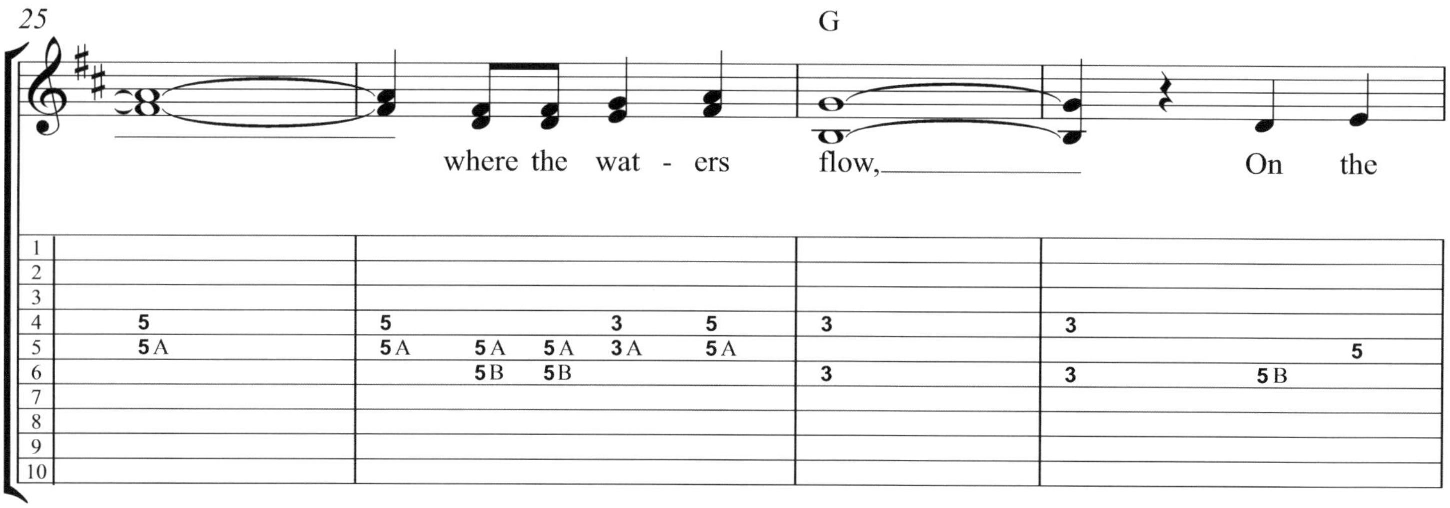

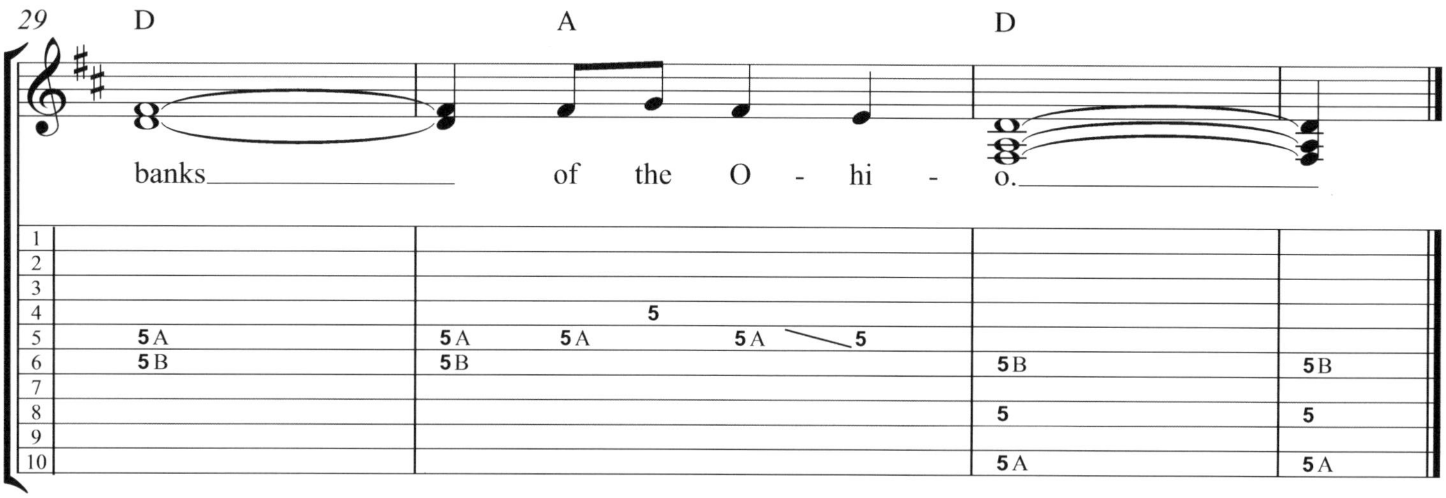

I held a knife against his breast
As into my arms he pressed
He cried "my love, don't you murder me
I'm not prepared for eternity"

I wandered home 'tween twelve and one
I cried, "My God, what have I done?"
I've killed the only man I love
He would not take me for his bride

And only say that you'll be mine
In no others' arms entwine
Down beside where the waters flow
Down by the banks of the Ohio

Precious Memories

The beautiful hymn, "Precious Memories" has been recorded by Aretha Franklin, Alan Jackson, Merle Haggard, and many others. Notice the occasional 3-note harmonies.

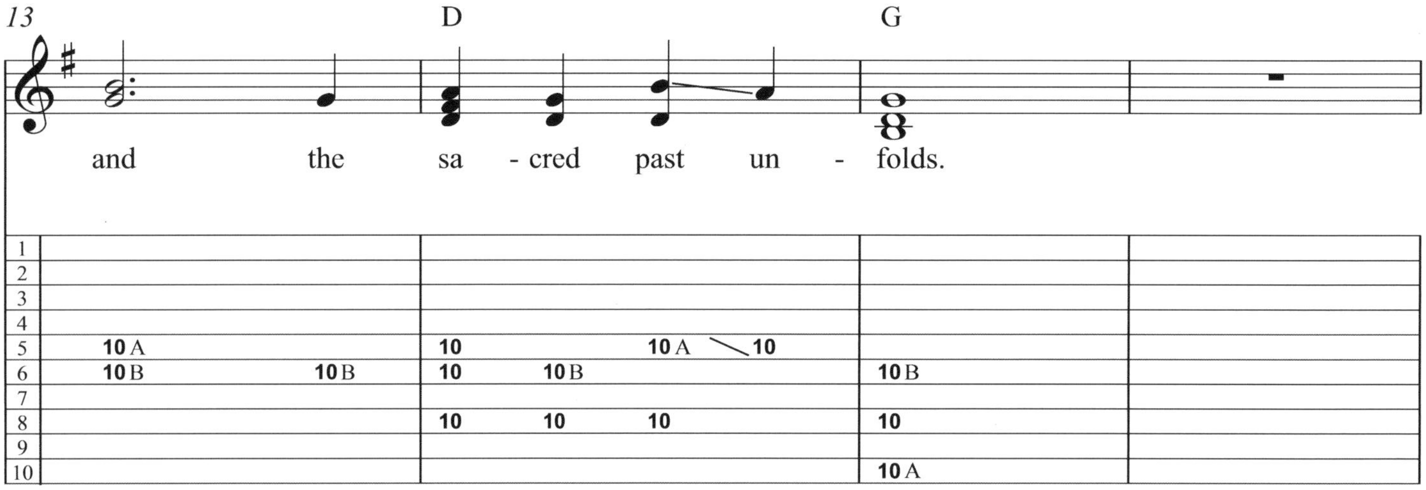
13
D
G
and the sa - cred past un - folds.

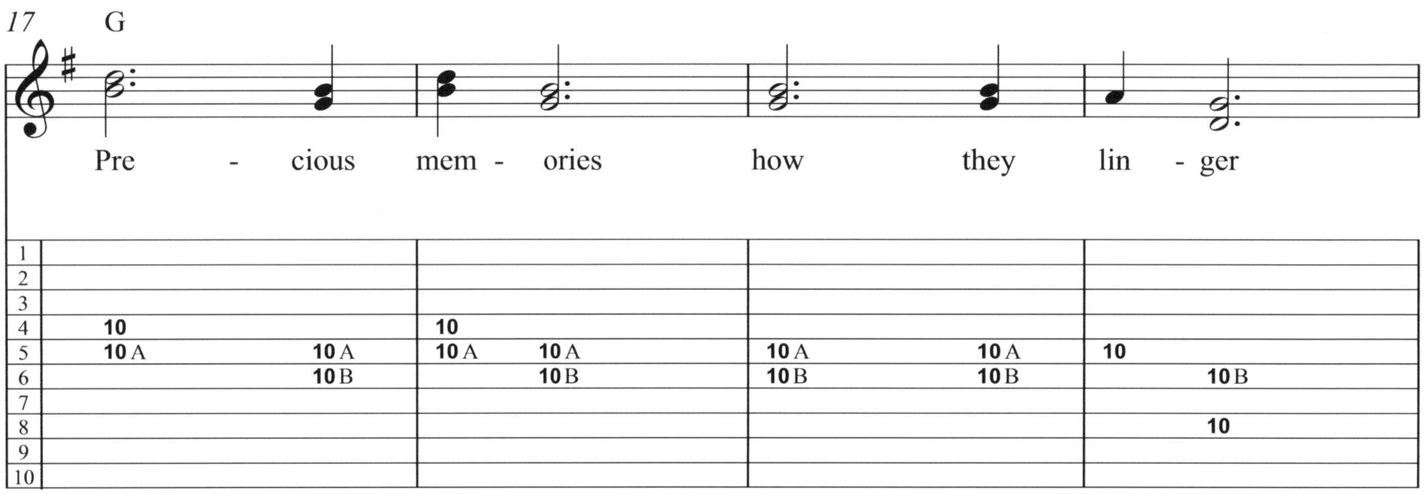
17
G
Pre - cious mem - ories how they lin - ger

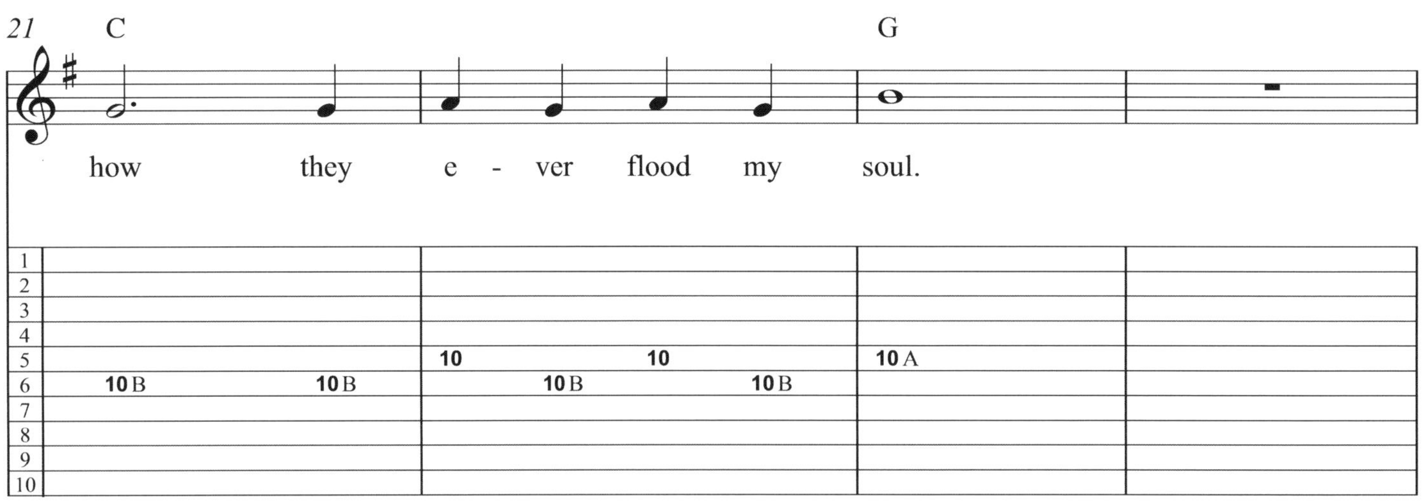
21
C
G
how they e - ver flood my soul.

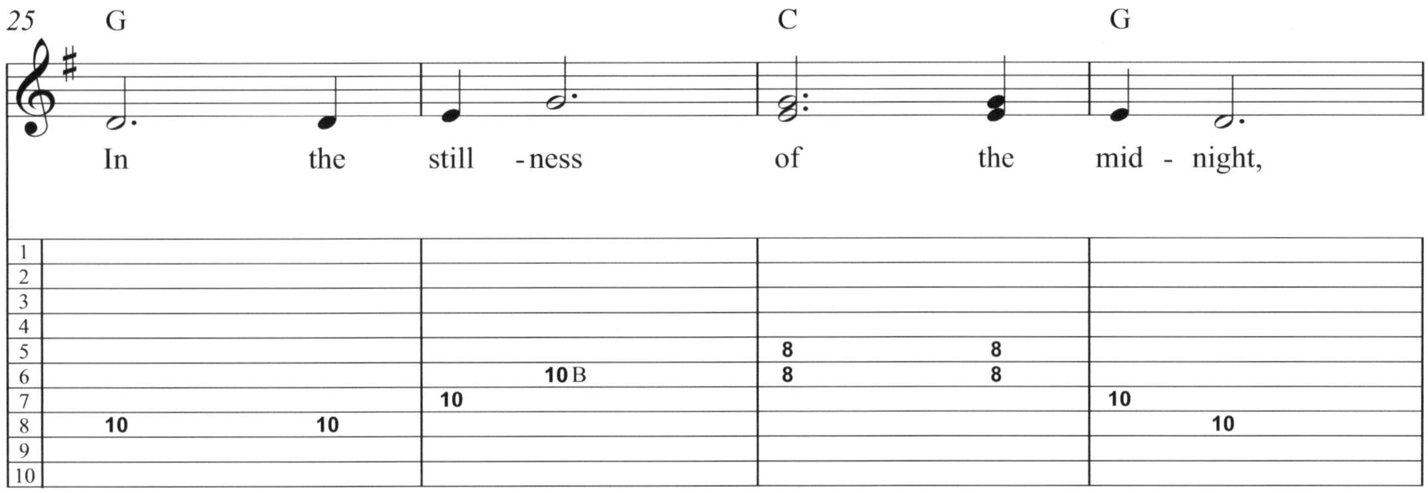

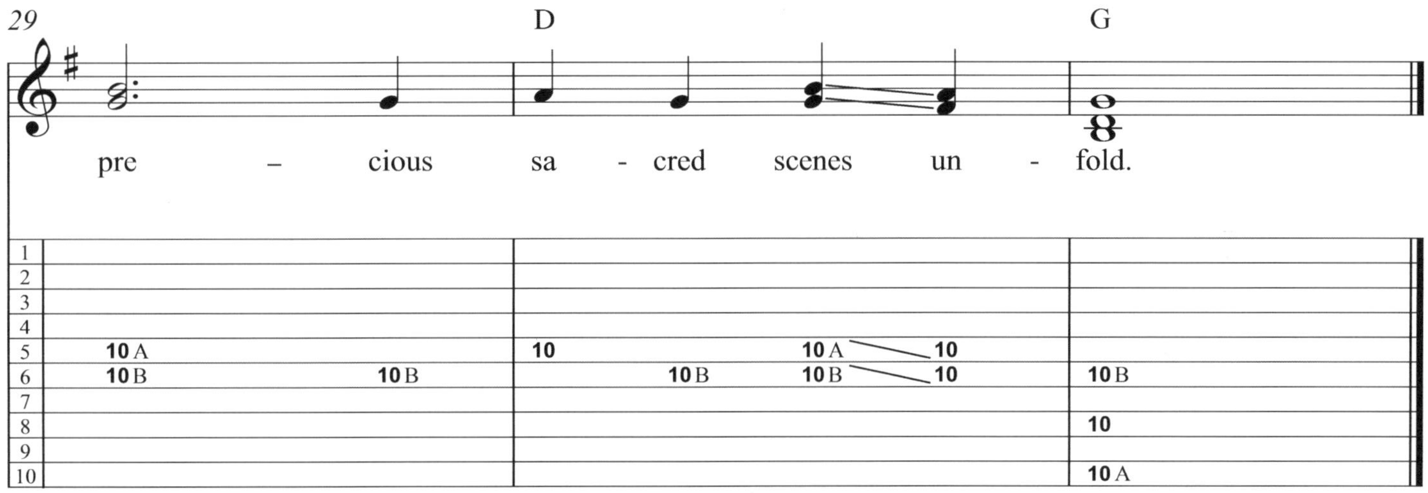

Precious father, loving mother
Fly across the lonely years
And old home scenes, of my childhood
In fond memory appears

Precious memories, how they linger
How they ever flood my soul
In the stillness, of the midnight
Precious sacred scenes unfold

I remember, mother prayin'
Father too, on bended knee
The sun is sinkin', shadows fallin'
But their prayers still follow me

Precious memories, how they linger
How they ever flood my soul
In the stillness, of the midnight
Precious sacred scenes unfold
Precious memories fill my soul

Red River Valley

The American cowboy song, "Red River Valley" has been performed by numerous artists, including Marty Robbins, Pete Seeger and Suzy Bogguss.

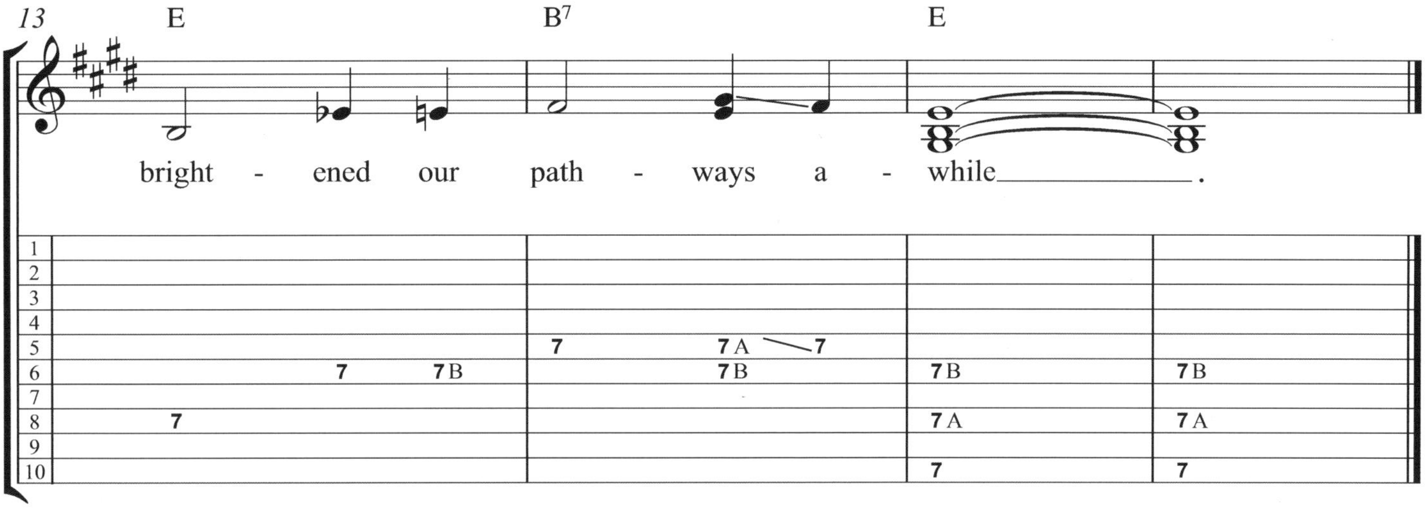

Do you think of the valley you're leavin'
Oh how lonely and dreary it will be
Do you think of the fond heart you're breakin'
And the sadness you've cast over me

For a long time my dear, I've been waiting
For the words that you never would say
And alas my poor heart you are breakin'

For they tell me you're goin' away
As you go to your home by the ocean
May you never forget those sweet hours
That we spent in the Red River Valley
And the love we exchanged mid the flowers

Come and sit by my side if you love me
Do not hasten to bid me adieu
But remember the Red River Valley
And the one that has loved you so true

Down in the Valley

Burl Ives, Andy Griffith and Glen Campbell are among the artists who have recorded this beautiful song "Down in the Valley". Strive for balance when playing the 3-note chords.

13
Hear the wind blow dear Hear the wind
17 G
blow Late in the eve -
21 C
ning hear the wind blow

20

Will the Circle Be Unbroken

"Will the Circle Be Unbroken" is a popular Christian hymn written in the early 1900's. It has been recorded by many artists including Johnny Cash, Ricky Skaggs, The Carter Family, and The Nitty Gritty Dirt Band.

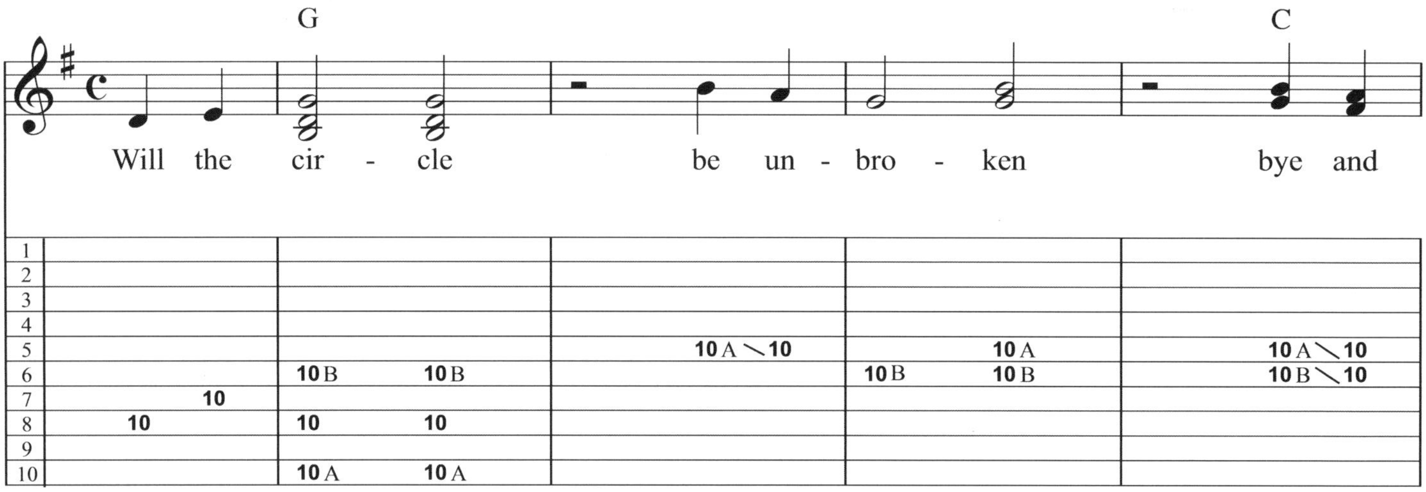

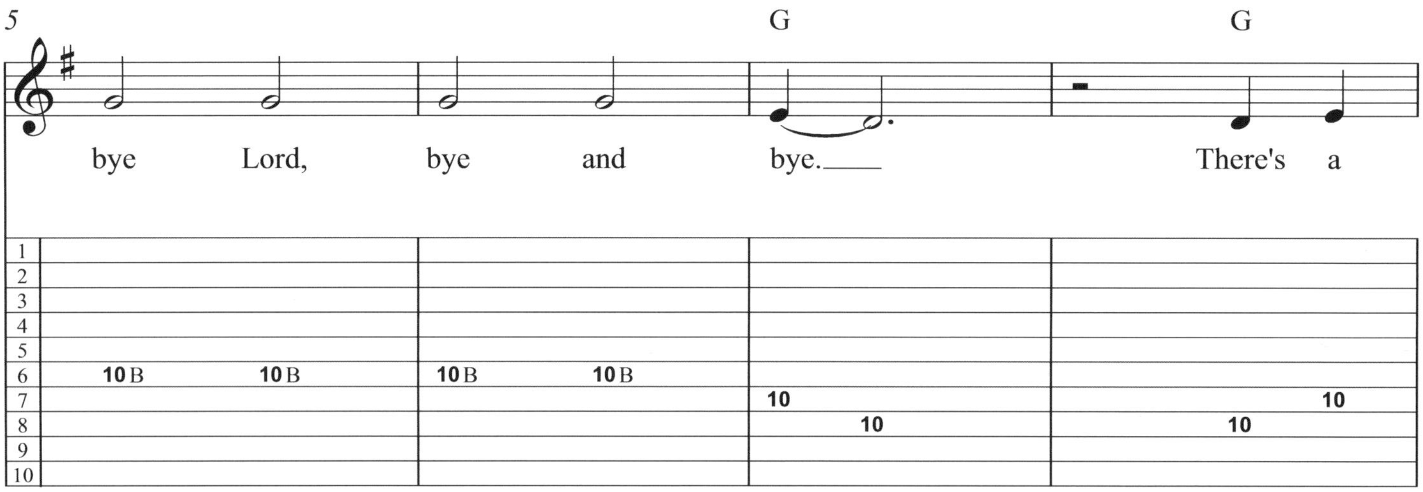

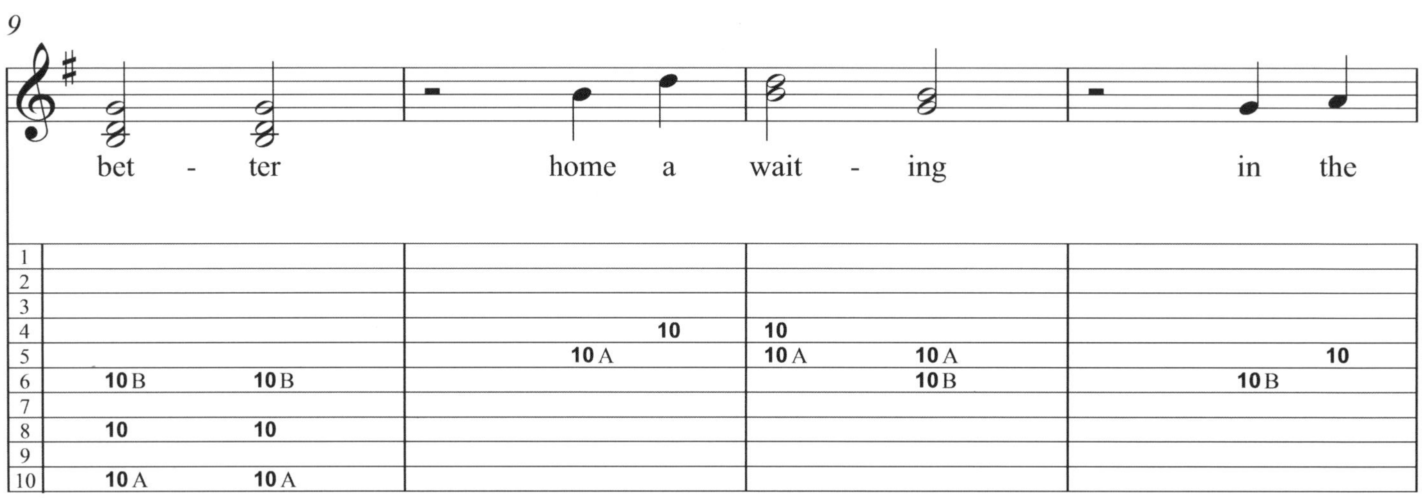

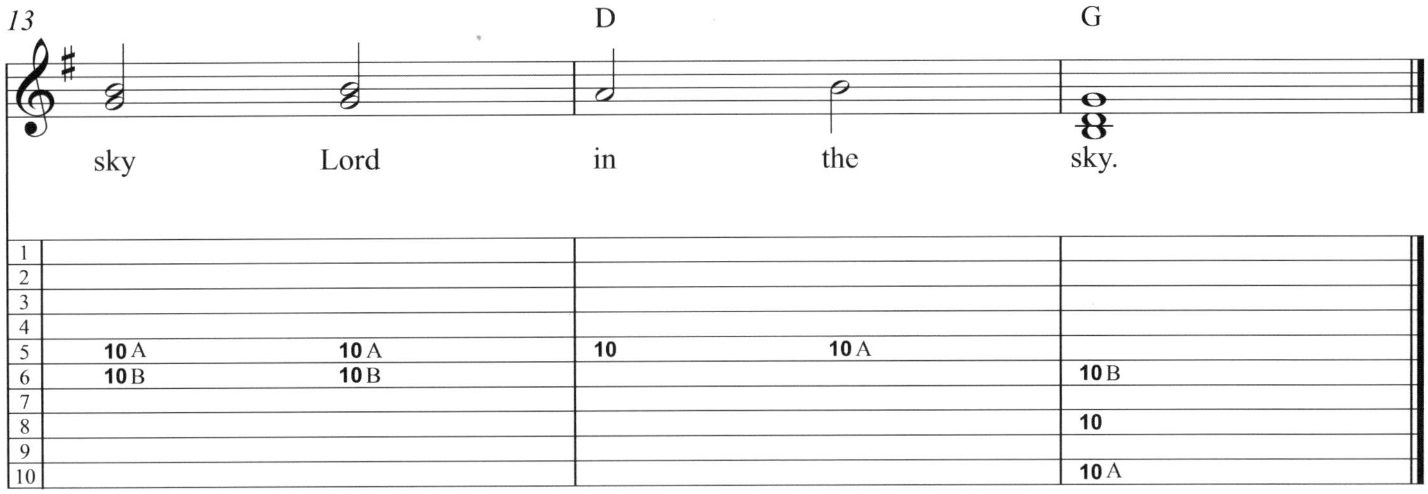
13
D
G
sky
Lord
in
the
sky.

About The Authors

John Hartin

John Hartin is widely known as the architect of the Country and Bluegrass music degree program at South Plains College in Levelland, Texas. Under John's leadership, the program became known worldwide, and has many famous graduates. John holds a Bachelor's degree from Briar Cliff University and a Masters from Wayland Baptist University. He has been inducted into the Buddy Holly Terrace Hall of Fame, the West Texas Hall of Fame, and both the Nebraska and Iowa Rock and Roll Halls of Fame. He has been a member of the Mel Bay Advisory Board, as well as the Commercial Music Advisory Board at South Plains College. John retired after 28 successful years at South Plains College and is now a partner at Texas Music Supply where he still teaches students every week on guitar, pedal steel, banjo, Dobro®, and mandolin.

Chet Hartin

Chester "Chet" Travis Hartin - was named after two great country guitarists (Chet Atkins and Merle Travis). Chet started playing gigs when he was fourteen and hasn't stopped. An accomplished bass and keyboard player, he's always learning a new instrument (steel guitar, accordion, banjo, mandolin, bagpipes, etc). He appears on several albums and has been very active in the New York and Chicago music scenes. When not playing music, you can usually find him on a computer doing his second favorite thing - programming, in that capacity he's worked for several large firms, including CBS and Amazon Web Services.

Other Mel Bay Pedal and Lap Steel Books